THE OPEN

MERIDIAN

Crossing Aesthetics

Werner Hamacher

Editor

Translated by
Kevin Attell

*Stanford
University
Press*

*Stanford
California*

THE OPEN

Man and Animal

Giorgio Agamben

Open Secrets: Book

Stanford University Press
Stanford, California

The Open was originally published in Italian in 2002 under
the title *L'aperto: L'uomo e l'animale.* © 2002, Bollati
Boringhieri.

Printed in the United States of America on acid-free,
archival-quality paper

Library of Congress Cataloging-in-Publication Data

Agamben, Giorgio, 1942–
    [Aperto. English]
    The open : man and animal / Giorgio Agamben.
        p.   cm. — (Meridian, crossing aesthetics)
    Includes bibliographical references and index.
    ISBN 0-8047-4737-7 (cloth : alk. paper) —
    ISBN 0-8047-4738-5 (pbk. : alk. paper)
    1. Philosophical anthropology.   2. Human beings—
Animal nature.   I. Title.   II. Series: Meridian
(Stanford, Calif.)
BD450 .A3613 2004
128—DC22
                                        2003018253

Original Printing 2004

Typeset by Tim Roberts in 10.9/13 Adobe Garamond

Contents

Translator's Note

Wherever possible, I have quoted from published English translations of Agamben's French, German, Greek, Italian, and Latin sources. However, in order to maintain consistency in terminology throughout the text, and to better reflect Agamben's own translations of these sources, the published English versions have frequently been modified. Where no English edition is cited, the translation is mine.

Material included between braces in the text is my own, as are all substantive endnotes.

I would like to thank Courtney Booker, David Copenhafer, Sirietta Simoncini, Dana Stevens, and Giorgio Agamben for their generous help in preparing this translation.

THE OPEN

S'il n'existoit point d'animaux, la nature de l'homme serait encore plus incompréhensible.

{If animals did not exist, the nature of man would be even more incomprehensible.}

—Georges-Louis Buffon

Indigebant tamen eis, ad experimentalem cognitionem sumendam de naturis eorum.

{Yet they needed them in order to draw from their nature an experimental knowledge.}

—Thomas Aquinas

§ 1   Theriomorphous

> In the last three hours of the day, God sits and plays with the
> Leviathan, as is written: "you made the Leviathan in order to
> play with it."
>
> —Talmud, Avodah Zarah

In the Ambrosian Library in Milan there is a Hebrew Bible
from the thirteenth century that contains precious miniatures.
The last two pages of the third codex are entirely illustrated with
scenes of mystic and messianic inspiration. Page 135*v* depicts the
vision of Ezekiel, though without representing the chariot. In the
center are the seven heavens, the moon, the sun, and the stars, and
in the corners, standing out from a blue background, are the four
eschatological animals: the cock, the eagle, the ox, and the lion.
The last page (136*r*) is divided into halves. The upper half represents the three primeval animals: the bird Ziz (in the form of a
winged griffin), the ox Behemoth, and the great fish Leviathan,
immersed in the sea and coiled upon itself. The scene that inter-
ests us in particular here is the last in every sense, since it concludes the codex as well as the history of humanity. It represents
the messianic banquet of the righteous on the last day. Under the
shade of paradisiacal trees and cheered by the music of two play-
ers, the righteous, with crowned heads, sit at a richly laid table.
The idea that in the days of the Messiah the righteous, who for
their entire lives have observed the prescriptions of the Torah, will
feast on the meat of Leviathan and Behemoth without worrying
whether their slaughter has been kosher or not is perfectly familiar to the rabbinic tradition. What is surprising, however, is one
detail that we have not yet mentioned: beneath the crowns, the

miniaturist has represented the righteous not with human faces, but with unmistakably animal heads. Here, not only do we recognize the eschatological animals in the three figures on the right—the eagle's fierce beak, the red head of the ox, and the lion's head—but the other two righteous ones in the image also display the grotesque features of an ass and the profile of a leopard. And in turn the two musicians have animal heads as well—in particular the more visible one on the right, who plays a kind of fiddle and shows an inspired monkey's face.

Why are the representatives of concluded humanity depicted with animal heads? Scholars who have addressed the question have not yet found a convincing explanation. According to Zofia Ameisenowa, who has dedicated a broad investigation to the subject, in which she attempts to apply the methods of the Warburgian school to Jewish materials, the images of the righteous with animal features are to be traced back to Gnostic-astrological representations of the theriomorphous decans, by way of the Gnostic doctrine in which the bodies of the righteous (or, better, the spiritual), ascending through the heavens after death, are transformed into stars and identified with the powers that govern each heaven.[1]

According to the rabbinic tradition, however, the righteous in question are not dead at all; they are, on the contrary, the representatives of the remnant {*resto*; also "rest," "remainder"} of Israel, that is, of the righteous who are still alive at the moment of the Messiah's coming. As we read in the Apocalypse of Baruch 29:4, "And Behemoth will appear from its land, and the Leviathan will rise from the sea: the two monsters which I formed on the fifth day of creation and which I have kept until that time shall be nourishment for all who are left."[2] Furthermore, the reason for the theriocephalous representation of the Gnostic archons and astrological decans is anything but settled for scholars, and it itself requires an explanation. In Manichean texts, each of the archons corresponds both to one part of the animal kingdom (bipeds, quadrupeds, birds, fish, reptiles) and, at the same time, to one of the "five natures" of the human body (bones, nerves, veins, flesh, skin), in such a way that the theriomorphous depiction of the archons refers directly back to the shadowy kinship between animal macrocosm and human microcosm.[3] In the Talmud, on the other hand, the passage of the tractate in which the Leviathan is mentioned as the food at the messianic banquet of the righteous occurs after a series of *Aggadoth* that seem to allude to a different economy of relations between animal and human. Moreover, the idea that animal nature will also be transfigured in the messianic kingdom is implicit in the messianic prophecy of Isaiah 11:6 (which so pleased Ivan Karamazov), where we read that "the wolf shall live with the sheep, / and the leopard lie down with the kid; / the calf and the young lion shall grow up together, / and a little child shall lead them."

It is not impossible, therefore, that in attributing an animal head to the remnant of Israel, the artist of the manuscript in the Ambrosian intended to suggest that on the last day, the relations between animals and men will take on a new form, and that man himself will be reconciled with his animal nature.

§ 2   Acephalous

Georges Bataille was so struck by the Gnostic effigies of animal-headed archons that he was able to see in the Cabinet des Médailles of the Bibliothèque Nationale that in 1930 he dedicated an article to them in his journal *Documents*. In Gnostic mythology, the archons are the demonic entities who create and govern the material world, in which the bright and spiritual elements are found mixed and imprisoned in those dark and bodily. The images that Bataille reproduced as evidence of the tendency of Gnostic "base materialism" to confuse human and bestial forms represent, according to his captions, "three archons with duck heads," one "panmorphous Iao," a "god with the legs of a man, the body of a serpent, and the head of a cock," and, finally, an "acephalous god topped with two animal heads."[1] Six years later, the cover of the first issue of the journal *Acéphale*, drawn by André Masson, showed a naked, headless human figure as the insignia of the "sacred conspiracy" which Bataille plotted with a small group of friends. Though man's evasion of his head ("Man has escaped from his head, as the condemned man from prison," reads the programmatic text)[2] does not necessarily entail a return to animality, the illustrations of issue 3–4 of the journal, in which the same naked figure from the first issue now bears a majestic bull's head, attest to an aporia which accompanies Bataille's entire project.

Indeed, one of the central issues of Kojève's lectures on Hegel, which Bataille attended at the École des Hautes Études, was the problem of the end of history and the figure that man and nature would assume in the posthistorical world, when the patient process of work and negation, by means of which the animal of the species *Homo sapiens* had become human, reached completion. In one of his characteristic gestures, Kojève dedicates to this problem only a footnote to the 1938–39 course.

> The disappearance of Man at the end of History is not a cosmic catastrophe: the natural World remains what it has been from all eternity. And it is not a biological catastrophe either: Man remains alive as animal in *harmony* with Nature or given Being. What disappears is Man properly so called—that is, Action negating the given, and Error, or, in general, the Subject *opposed* to the Object. In point of fact, the end of human Time or History—that is, the definitive annihilation of Man properly so called or of the free and historical Individual—means quite simply the cessation of Action in the strong sense of the term. Practically, this means: the disappearance of wars and bloody revolutions. And the disappearance of *Philosophy*; for since Man no longer changes himself essentially, there is no longer any reason to change the (true) principles which are at the basis of his knowledge of the World and of himself. But all the rest can be preserved indefinitely; art, love, play, etc., etc.; in short, everything that makes Man *happy*.[3]

The disagreement between Bataille and Kojève concerns just that "rest" {*resto*} that survives the death of man, who has become animal again at the end of history. What the pupil—who was, in fact, five years older than the teacher—could not accept at any cost was that "art, love, play," as well as laughter, ecstasy, luxury (which, wrapped in an aura of exceptionality, were at the center of *Acéphale*'s concerns, as well as those of the Collège de Sociologie two years later), ceased to be superhuman, negative, and sacred, in order simply to be given back to animal praxis. For the small group of forty-year-old initiates—who were not afraid to challenge the ridiculous by practicing "joy in the face of death" in the woods on the outskirts of Paris, nor later, in full European crisis, to play at being "sorcerer's apprentices" preaching the European peoples' return to the "old house of myth"—the acephalous being glimpsed for an instant in their privileged experiences might have been neither human nor divine, but in no case could it be animal.

Of course, at issue here was also the interpretation of Hegel, a terrain in which Kojève's authority was particularly threatening. If history is nothing but the patient dialectical work of negation, and man both the subject and the stakes in this negating action, then the completion of history necessarily entails the end of man, and the face of the wise man who, on the threshold of time, contemplates this end with satisfaction necessarily fades, as in the miniature in the Ambrosian, into an animal snout.

For this reason, in a letter to Kojève on December 6, 1937, Bataille has to wager on the idea of a "negativity with no use" {*negatività senza impiego*; also "unemployed negativity"}, that is, of a negativity that somehow survives the end of history and for which he can provide no proof other than his own life, "the open wound that is my life."

> I grant (as a likely supposition) that from now on history is concluded (except for the epilogue). However, I picture things differently. . . . If action ("doing") is—as Hegel says—negativity, the question arises as to whether the negativity of one who has "nothing more to do" disappears or remains in a state of "negativity with no use": personally, I can only decide in one way, being myself precisely this "negativity with no use" (I would not be able to define myself more precisely). I recognize that Hegel has foreseen such a possibility; at any rate he didn't situate it at the *end* of the process he described. I imagine that my life—or better yet, its aborting, the open wound that is my life—constitutes all by itself the refutation of Hegel's closed system.[4]

The end of history involves, then, an "epilogue" in which human negativity is preserved as a "remnant" in the form of eroticism, laughter, joy in the face of death. In the uncertain light of this epilogue, the wise man, sovereign and self-conscious, sees not animal heads passing again before his eyes, but rather the acephalous figures of the *hommes farouchement religieux*, "lovers," or "sorcerer's apprentices." The epilogue, however, would prove to be fragile. In 1939, with the war by now inevitable, a declaration

by the Collège de Sociologie betrays its impotence, denouncing
the passivity and absence of reaction in the face of war as a form
of massive "devirilization," in which men are transformed into a
sort of "conscious sheep resigned to the slaughterhouse."[5] Though
in a sense different from the one Kojève had in mind, men had
now truly become animals again.

§ 3   Snob

No animal can be a snob.

—Alexandre Kojève

In 1968, on the occasion of the second edition of the *Introduction*, by which time his disciple-rival had been dead six years, Kojève returns to the problem of man's becoming animal. And once again, he does so in the form of a footnote added to the footnote in the first edition (if the text of the *Introduction* is essentially composed from the notes collected by Queneau, then the footnotes are the only part of the text surely from Kojève's hand). That first note, he observes, was ambiguous, because if we accept that at the end of history man "properly so called" must disappear, then we cannot coherently expect that "all the rest" (art, love, play) can remain indefinitely.

> If Man becomes an animal again, his arts, his loves, and his play must also become purely "natural" again. Hence it would have to be admitted that after the end of History, men would construct their edifices and works of art as birds build their nests and spiders spin their webs, would perform musical concerts after the fashion of frogs and cicadas, would play as young animals play, and would indulge in love like adult beasts. But one cannot then say that all this "makes Man *happy*." One would have to say that post-historical animals of the species *Homo sapiens* (which will live amidst abundance and complete security) will be *content* as a result of their artistic, erotic, and playful behavior, inasmuch as, by definition, they will be contented with it.[1]

The definitive annihilation of man in the proper sense, however, must also entail the disappearance of human language, and its substitution by mimetic or sonic signals comparable to the language of bees. But in that case, Kojève argues, not only would philosophy—that is, the love of wisdom—disappear, but so would the very possibility of any wisdom as such.

At this point the note articulates a series of theses on the end of history and on the present state of the world, in which it is impossible to distinguish between absolute seriousness and an equally absolute irony. We thus learn that in the years immediately following the writing of the first note (1946), the author understood that the "Hegelo-Marxist end of history" was not a future event but something already completed. After the battle of Jena, the vanguard of humanity virtually reached the end of man's historical evolution. Everything that followed—including two world wars, Nazism, and the sovietization of Russia—represented nothing but a process of accelerated alignment of the rest of the world with the position of the most advanced European countries. Yet now, repeated trips to the United States and Russia, taken between 1948 and 1958 (by which time Kojève had become a high functionary in the French government), convinced him that, on the road toward reaching the posthistorical condition, "the Russians and the Chinese are only Americans who are still poor but are rapidly proceeding to become richer," while the United States has already reached the "final stage of Marxist 'communism.'"[2] This then led him to the conclusion that

> the "American way of life" was the type of life proper to the post-historical period, the current presence of the United States in the World prefiguring the future "eternal present" of all humanity. Thus, man's return to animality appeared no longer as a possibility that was yet to come, but as a certainty that was already present.[3]

In 1959, however, a trip to Japan brought about a further shift in perspective. In Japan, Kojève was able to see with his own eyes a society which, though living in a condition of posthistory, had nevertheless not ceased to be "human."

"Post-historical" Japanese civilization undertook ways diametrically opposed to the "American way." No doubt, there were no longer in Japan any Religion, Morals, or Politics in the "European" or "historical" sense of these words. But *Snobbery* in its pure state created disciplines negating the "natural" or "animal" given which in effectiveness far surpassed those that arose, in Japan or elsewhere, from "historical" Action—that is, from warlike and revolutionary Struggles or from forced Work. To be sure, the peaks (equalled nowhere else) of specifically Japanese snobbery—the Noh theatre, the ceremony of tea, and the art of bouquets of flowers—were and still remain the exclusive prerogative of the nobles and the rich. But in spite of persistent economic and social inequalities, all Japanese without exception are currently in a position to live according to totally *formalized* values— that is, values completely empty of all "human" content in the "historical" sense. Thus, in the extreme, every Japanese is in principle capable of committing, from pure snobbery, a perfectly "gratuitous" *suicide* (the classical sword of the samurai can be replaced with an airplane or a torpedo), which has nothing to do with the *risk* of life in a Struggle waged for the sake of "historical" values that have social or political content. This seems to allow one to believe that the recently begun interaction between Japan and the Western World will finally lead not to a rebarbarization of the Japanese but to a "Japanization" of the Westerners (including the Russians).

Now, since no animal can be a snob, every "Japanized" post-historical period would be specifically human. Hence there would be no "definitive annihilation of Man properly so called," as long as there were animals of the species *Homo sapiens* that could serve as the "natural" support for what is human in men.[4]

The farcical tone, for which Bataille reproached his teacher every time Kojève attempted to describe the posthistorical condition, reaches its peak in this note. Not only is the "American way of life" equated with an animal life, but man's survival of history in the form of Japanese snobbery resembles a more elegant (if, perhaps, parodic) version of that "negativity with no use" that Bataille sought to define, in his certainly more ingenuous way, and that to Kojève's eyes must have seemed in bad taste.

Let us try to reflect on the theoretical implications of this posthistorical figure of the human. First of all, humanity's survival of its historical drama seems to introduce—between history and its end—a fringe of ultrahistory that recalls the messianic reign of one thousand years that, in both the Jewish and Christian traditions, will be established on Earth between the last messianic event and the eternal life (which is not surprising in a thinker who had dedicated his first work to the philosophy of Solov'yev, itself imbued with messianic and eschatological themes). But what is decisive is that in this ultrahistorical fringe, man's remaining human presumes the survival of animals of the species *Homo sapiens* that must function as his support. For in Kojève's reading of Hegel, man is not a biologically defined species, nor is he a substance given once and for all; he is, rather, a field of dialectical tensions always already cut by internal caesurae that every time separate—at least virtually—"anthropophorous" animality and the humanity which takes bodily form in it. Man exists historically only in this tension; he can be human only to the degree that he transcends and transforms the anthropophorous animal which supports him, and only because, through the action of negation, he is capable of mastering and, eventually, destroying his own animality (it is in this sense that Kojève can write that "man is a fatal disease of the animal").[5]

But what becomes of the animality of man in posthistory? What relation is there between the Japanese snob and his animal body, and between this and the acephalous creature glimpsed by Bataille? Kojève, however, privileges the aspect of negation and death in the relation between man and the anthropophorous animal, and he seems not to see the process by which, on the contrary, man (or the State for him) in modernity begins to care for his own animal life, and by which natural life becomes the stakes in what Foucault called biopower. Perhaps the body of the anthropophorous animal (the body of the slave) is the unresolved remnant that idealism leaves as an inheritance to thought, and the aporias of the philosophy of our time coincide with the aporias of this body that is irreducibly drawn and divided between animality and humanity.

§ 4 *Mysterium disiunctionis*

For anyone undertaking a genealogical study of the concept of "life" in our culture, one of the first and most instructive observations to be made is that the concept never gets defined as such. And yet, this thing that remains indeterminate gets articulated and divided time and again through a series of caesurae and oppositions that invest it with a decisive strategic function in domains as apparently distant as philosophy, theology, politics, and—only later—medicine and biology. That is to say, everything happens as if, in our culture, life were *what cannot be defined, yet, precisely for this reason, must be ceaselessly articulated and divided*.

In the history of Western philosophy, this strategic articulation of the concept of life has a foundational moment. It is the moment in *De anima* when, from among the various senses of the term "to live," Aristotle isolates the most general and separable one.

> It is through life that what has soul in it {*l'animale*} differs from what has not {*l'inanimato*}.[1] Now this term "to live" has more than one sense, and provided any one alone of these is found in a thing we say that the thing is living—viz. thinking, sensation, local movement and rest, or movement in the sense of nutrition, decay and growth. Hence we think of all species of plants also as living, for they are observed to possess in themselves a principle and potentiality through which they grow and decay in opposite directions. . . . This principle can be sep-

arated from the others, but not they from it—in mortal beings at
least. The fact is obvious in plants; for it is the only psychic potentiality {*potenza dell'anima*} they possess. Thus, it is through this principle that life belongs to living things. . . . By nutritive power [*threp-
tikon*] we mean that part of the soul which is common also to plants.[2]

It is important to observe that Aristotle in no way defines what
life is: he limits himself to breaking it down, by isolating the nutritive function, in order then to rearticulate it in a series of distinct
and correlated faculties or potentialities (nutrition, sensation,
thought). Here we see at work that principle of foundation which
constitutes the strategic device par excellence of Aristotle's
thought. It consists in reformulating every question concerning
"what something is" as a question concerning "through what [*dia
ti*] something belongs to another thing." To ask why a certain
being is called living means to seek out the foundation by which
living belongs to this being. That is to say, among the various senses of the term "to live," one must be separated from the others and
settle to the bottom, becoming the principle by which life can be
attributed to a certain being. In other words, what has been separated and divided (in this case nutritive life) is precisely what—in
a sort of *divide et impera*—allows the construction of the unity of
life as the hierarchical articulation of a series of functional faculties and oppositions.

The isolation of nutritive life (which the ancient commentators
will already call vegetative) constitutes in every sense a fundamental event for Western science. When Bichat, many centuries later,
in his *Recherches physiologiques sur la vie et la mort*, distinguishes
between "animal life," which is defined by its relation to an external world, and "organic life," which is nothing other than a
"habitual succession of assimilation and excretion,"[3] it is again
Aristotle's nutritive life that marks out the obscure background
from which the life of the higher animals gets separated.
According to Bichat, it is as if two "animals" lived together in
every higher organism: *l'animal existant au-dedans*—whose life,
which Bichat defines as "organic," is merely the repetition of, so to

speak, blind and unconscious functions (the circulation of blood, respiration, assimilation, excretion, etc.)—and *l'animal existant au-dehors*—whose life, for Bichat the only one that merits the name of "animal," is defined through its relation to the external world. In man, these two animals live together, but they do not coincide; the internal animal's {*animale-di-dentro*} organic life begins in the fetus before animal life does, and in aging and in the final death throes it survives the death of the external animal {*animale-di-fuori*}.

It is hardly necessary to mention the strategic importance that the identification of this split between the functions of vegetative life and the functions of relational life has had in the history of modern medicine. The successes of modern surgery and anesthesia are founded upon, among other things, just this possibility of dividing and, at the same time, articulating Bichat's two animals. And as Foucault has shown, when the modern State, starting in the seventeenth century, began to include the care of the population's life as one of its essential tasks, thus transforming its politics into biopolitics, it was primarily by means of a progressive generalization and redefinition of the concept of vegetative life (now coinciding with the biological heritage of the nation) that the State would carry out its new vocation. And still today, in discussions about the definition *ex lege* of the criteria for clinical death, it is a further identification of this bare life—detached from any brain activity and, so to speak, from any subject—which decides whether a certain body can be considered alive or must be abandoned to the extreme vicissitude of transplantation.

The division of life into vegetal and relational, organic and animal, animal and human, therefore passes first of all as a mobile border within living man, and without this intimate caesura the very decision of what is human and what is not would probably not be possible. It is possible to oppose man to other living things, and at the same time to organize the complex—and not always edifying—economy of relations between men and animals, only because something like an animal life has been separated within man, only because his distance and proximity to the animal have been measured and recognized first of all in the closest and most intimate place.

But if this is true, if the caesura between the human and the animal passes first of all within man, then it is the very question of man—and of "humanism"—that must be posed in a new way. In our culture, man has always been thought of as the articulation and conjunction of a body and a soul, of a living thing and a *logos*, of a natural (or animal) element and a supernatural or social or divine element. We must learn instead to think of man as what results from the incongruity of these two elements, and investigate not the metaphysical mystery of conjunction, but rather the practical and political mystery of separation. What is man, if he is always the place—and, at the same time, the result—of ceaseless divisions and caesurae? It is more urgent to work on these divisions, to ask in what way—within man—has man been separated from non-man, and the animal from the human, than it is to take positions on the great issues, on so-called human rights and values. And perhaps even the most luminous sphere of our relations with the divine depends, in some way, on that darker one which separates us from the animal.

§ 5 Physiology of the Blessed

What is this Paradise, but a tavern of ceaseless gorging and a
brothel of perpetual bawdiness?

— William of Auvergne

It is particularly instructive, from this point of view, to read
medieval treatises on the integrity and quality of the body of the
resurrected. The problem that the Fathers had to confront first of
all was that of the resurrected body's identity with the body of the
man in life. For the identity of these two bodies seemed to imply
that all the matter that had belonged to the body of the dead person must come back to life and take its place once again in the
blessed organism. But this is precisely where difficulties arose. If,
for example, a thief—who had later repented and been
redeemed—had had a hand amputated, would the hand be
rejoined to the body at the moment of resurrection? And the rib
of Adam, asks Thomas, from which the body of Eve had been
formed, will it be resurrected in Eve's body or in Adam's?
Moreover, according to medieval science food is transformed into
living flesh; in the case of an anthropophagus who has fed on
other human bodies, this would have to mean that in the resurrection one single matter would be reintegrated into several indi-
viduals. And what about hair and fingernails? And sperm, sweat,
milk, urine, and other secretions? If the intestines are resurrected,
argues one theologian, they must come back either empty or full.
If full, this means that even filth will rise again; if empty, then we
will have an organ which no longer has any natural function.

The problem of the identity and integrity of the risen body thus

17

quickly becomes that of the physiology of blessed life. How should the vital functions of the paradisiacal body be conceived? In order to orient themselves on such an uneven ground, the Fathers had a useful paradigm at their disposal: the Edenic body of Adam and Eve before the Fall. "What God planted in the delights of eternal and blessed happiness," writes Scotus Erigena, "is human nature itself created in His image and likeness."[1] From this perspective, the physiology of the blessed body could appear as a restoration of the Edenic body, the archetype of uncorrupted human nature. This, however, entailed some consequences which the Fathers were not ready to fully accept. To be sure, as Augustine had explained, Adam's sexuality before the Fall did not resemble ours, since his sexual parts could be moved voluntarily just like hands or feet, so that sexual union could occur without the need of any concupiscent stimulus. And Adamic nourishment was infinitely more noble than ours, for it consisted solely of the fruits from the trees of Paradise. But even so, how should we conceive of the use of the sexual parts—or even simply of food—on the part of the blessed?

For if it were allowed that the risen would reproduce by means of sexuality and nourish themselves with food, this would mean that the number and bodily form of men would grow or change infinitely, and that there would be countless blessed ones who had never lived before the resurrection and whose humanity would therefore be impossible to define. The two principal functions of animal life—nutrition and generation—are directed to the preservation of the individual and of the species; but after the resurrection humanity would have reached its preordained number, and, in the absence of death, these two functions would be entirely useless. Furthermore, if the risen were to continue to eat and reproduce, not only would Paradise not be big enough to contain them all, but it would not even hold their excrement—thus justifying William of Auvergne's ironic invective: *maledicta Paradisus in qua tantum cacatur!* {Cursed Paradise in which there is so much defecation!}

There was, however, a still more insidious doctrine that maintained that the risen would use sex and food not for the preservation of the individual or of the species, but rather (since beatitude consists in the perfect operation of human nature) so that in Paradise all of man, his bodily as well as his spiritual powers, would be blessed. Against these heretics—whom he likens to Muhammadans and Jews—Thomas, in the questions *De resurrectione* that were added to the *Summa theologica*, forcefully reaffirms the exclusion of the *usus venereorum et ciborum* from Paradise. The resurrection, he teaches, is directed not to the perfection of man's natural life, but only to that final perfection which is contemplative life.

> Those natural operations which are arranged for the purpose of either achieving or preserving the primary perfection of human nature will not exist in the resurrection. . . . And since to eat, drink, sleep, and beget pertain to . . . the primary perfection of nature, such things will not exist in the resurrection.[2]

The same author who had shortly before affirmed that man's sin had in no way changed the nature and condition of animals, now proclaims unreservedly that animal life is excluded from Paradise, that blessed life is in no case an animal life. Consequently, even plants and animals will not find a place in Paradise: "they will corrupt both in their whole and in their parts."[3] In the body of the resurrected, the animal functions will remain "idle and empty" exactly as Eden, according to medieval theology, remains empty of all human life after the expulsion of Adam and Eve. All flesh will not be saved, and in the physiology of the blessed, the divine *oikonomia* of salvation leaves an unredeemable remnant.

§ 6 *Cognitio experimentalis*

We can, then, advance some provisional hypotheses about what makes the representation of the righteous with animal heads in the miniature in the Ambrosian so enigmatic. The messianic end of history or the completion of the divine *oikonomia* of salvation defines a critical threshold, at which the difference between animal and human, which is so decisive for our culture, threatens to vanish. That is to say, the relation between man and animal marks the boundary of an essential domain, in which historical inquiry must necessarily confront that fringe of ultrahistory which cannot be reached without making recourse to first philosophy. It is as if determining the border between human and animal were not just one question among many discussed by philosophers and theologians, scientists and politicians, but rather a fundamental metaphysico-political operation in which alone something like "man" can be decided upon and produced. If animal life and human life could be superimposed perfectly, then neither man nor animal—and, perhaps, not even the divine—would any longer be thinkable. For this reason, the arrival at posthistory necessarily entails the reactualization of the prehistoric threshold at which that border had been defined. Paradise calls Eden back into question.

In a passage of the *Summa* bearing the significant heading *Utrum Adam in statu innocentiae animalibus dominaretur* {Whether Adam in the State of Innocence Had Mastery Over the

Animals}, Thomas seems for a moment to come close to the center of the problem, evoking a "cognitive experiment" whose place would be in the relationship between man and animal.

> In the state of innocence [he writes] men did not have any bodily need of animals. Neither for clothing, since they were naked and not ashamed, there being no motions of inordinate concupiscence; nor for food, since they fed on the trees of Paradise; nor for means of transport, their bodies being strong enough for that purpose. Yet they needed them in order to draw from their nature an experimental knowledge [*Indigebant tamen eis, ad experimentalem cognitionem sumendam de naturis eorum*]. This is signified by the fact that God led the animals before man, that he might give them a name that designated their nature.[1]

We must try to grasp what is at stake in this *cognitio experimentalis*. Perhaps not only theology and philosophy but also politics, ethics, and jurisprudence are drawn and suspended in the difference between man and animal. The cognitive experiment at issue in this difference ultimately concerns the nature of man—or, more precisely, the production and definition of this nature; it is an experiment *de hominis natura*. When the difference vanishes and the two terms collapse upon each other—as seems to be happening today—the difference between being and the nothing, licit and illicit, divine and demonic also fades away, and in its place something appears for which we seem to lack even a name. Perhaps concentration and extermination camps are also an experiment of this sort, an extreme and monstrous attempt to decide between the human and the inhuman, which has ended up dragging the very possibility of the distinction to its ruin.

§ 7   Taxonomies

Cartesius certe non vidit simios.
{Surely Descartes never saw an ape.}

—Carolus Linnaeus

Linnaeus, the founder of modern scientific taxonomy, had a weakness for apes. It is likely that he had had the occasion to see some up close during a period of study in Amsterdam, which was then an important center for trade in exotic animals. Later, having returned to Sweden and become the royal chief physician, he gathered together in Uppsala a small zoo that included various species of apes and monkeys, among which it is said he was particularly fond of a Barbary ape named Diana. The idea that apes, like the other *bruta,* were essentially different from man in that they lacked a soul was something he was not ready to concede easily to the theologians. In a note to the *Systema naturae* he dismisses the Cartesian theory that conceived of animals as if they were *automata mechanica* with the vexed statement: "surely Descartes never saw an ape." In a later writing bearing the title *Menniskans Cousiner,* "Man's Cousins," he explains how difficult it is to identify the specific difference between the anthropoid apes and man from the point of view of natural science. Not that he does not see the clear difference that separates man from beast on the moral and religious level:

> Man is the animal which the Creator found worthy of honoring with such a marvelous mind and which he wanted to adopt as His favorite, reserving for him a nobler existence; God even sent His only son to save him.

23

But all this, he concludes,

> belongs to another forum; just as the shoemaker sticks to his last, I must remain in my workshop and consider man and his body as a naturalist, who hardly knows a single distinguishing mark which separates man from the apes, save for the fact that the latter have an empty space between their canines and their other teeth.[1]

The peremptory gesture with which, in the *Systema naturae*, he assigns *Homo* to the order of the *Anthropomorpha* (which, from the tenth edition of 1758, will be called *Primates*) alongside *Simia*, *Lemur*, and *Vespertilio* (the bat) cannot, therefore, be a surprise. Besides, despite the polemics that his gesture did not fail to provoke, in a certain sense the issue was in the air. Already in 1693, John Ray had distinguished the group of the *Anthropomorpha*, the "manlike" animals, among the quadrupeds. And in general, in the Ancien Régime the boundaries of man are much more uncertain and fluctuating than they will appear in the nineteenth century, after the development of the human sciences. Up until the eighteenth century, language—which would become man's identifying characteristic par excellence—jumps across orders and classes, for it is suspected that even birds can talk. A witness as credible as John Locke refers to the story of the Prince of Nassau's parrot—which was able to hold a conversation and respond to questions "like a reasonable creature"—more or less as a certainty. And even the physical demarcation between man and the other species entailed zones of indifference in which it was not possible to assign certain identities. A serious scientific work such as Peter Artedi's *Ichthiologia* (1738) still listed sirens next to seals and sea lions, and Linnaeus himself, in his *Pan Europaeus*, classifies sirens—which the Danish anatomist Caspar Bartholin called *Homo marinus*—together with man and apes. On the other hand, the boundary between the anthropoid apes and certain primitive populations was also anything but clear. The first description of an orangutan by the doctor Nicolas Tulp in 1641 emphasizes the human aspects of this *Homo sylvestris* (which is the meaning of the Malay expression *orang-utan*); and we must wait until Edward Tyson's treatise *Orang-Outang, sive Homo Sylvestris: or, the Anatomy of a Pygmie*

(1699) for the physical difference between ape and man to first be posed on the solid grounds of comparative anatomy. Though this work is considered a sort of incunabulum of primatology, the creature that Tyson calls a "Pygmie" (and which is anatomically distinguished from man by thirty-four characteristics, from apes and monkeys by forty-eight) nevertheless represents for him a sort of "intermediate animal" between ape and man, to whom it stands in a relation symmetrically opposite to that of the angel.

> The animal of which I have given the Anatomy, [writes Tyson in the dedication to Lord Falconer] coming nearest to Mankind; seems the Nexus of the Animal and the Rational, as your Lordship, and those of your High Rank and Order for Knowledge and Wisdom, approaching nearest to that kind of Beings which is next above us; Connect the Visible, and Invisible World.[2]

And one look at the complete title of the treatise is enough to realize how the boundaries of the human were still threatened not only by real animals but also by creatures from mythology: *Orang-Outang, sive Homo Sylvestris: or, the Anatomy of a Pygmie Compared with that of a Monkey, an Ape, and a Man. To which is added, a Philological Essay Concerning the Pygmies, the Cynocephali, the Satyrs, and Sphinges of the Ancients. Wherein it Will Appear that They are all Either Apes or Monkeys, and not Men, as Formerly Pretended.*

In truth, Linnaeus's genius consists not so much in the resoluteness with which he places man among the primates as in the irony with which he does not record—as he does with the other species—any specific identifying characteristic next to the generic name *Homo*, only the old philosophical adage: *nosce te ipsum* {know yourself}. Even in the tenth edition, when the complete denomination becomes *Homo sapiens*, all evidence suggests that the new epithet does not represent a description, but that it is only a simplification of that adage, which, moreover, maintains its position next to the term *Homo*. It is worth reflecting on this taxonomic anomaly, which assigns not a given, but rather an imperative as a specific difference.

An analysis of the *Introitus* that opens the *Systema* leaves no doubts about the sense Linnaeus attributed to his maxim: man has no specific identity other than the *ability* to recognize himself. Yet to define the human not through any *nota characteristica*, but rather through his self-knowledge, means that man is the being which recognizes itself as such, that *man is the animal that must recognize itself as human to be human*. Indeed, Linnaeus writes that, at the moment of birth, nature has thrown man "bare upon the bare earth," unable to know, speak, walk, or feed himself, unless all this is taught to him (*Nudus in nuda terra . . . cui scire nichil sine doctrina; non fari, non ingredi, non vesci, non aliud naturae sponte*). He becomes himself only if he raises himself above man (*o quam contempta res est homo, nisi supra humana se erexerit*).[3]

In a letter to a critic, Johann Georg Gmelin, who objected that in the *Systema* man seemed to have been created in the image of the ape, Linnaeus responds by offering the sense of his maxim: "And nevertheless man recognizes himself. Perhaps I should remove those words. Yet I ask you and the entire world to show me a generic difference between ape and man which is consistent with the principles of natural history. I most certainly do not know of any."[4] The notes for a reply to another critic, Theodor Klein, show how far Linnaeus was willing to push the irony implicit in the formula *Homo sapiens*. Those who, like Klein, do not recognize themselves in the position that the *Systema* has assigned to man should apply the *nosce te ipsum* to themselves; in not knowing how to recognize themselves as man, they have placed themselves among the apes.

Homo sapiens, then, is neither a clearly defined species nor a substance; it is, rather, a machine or device for producing the recognition of the human. In line with the taste of the epoch, the anthropogenic (or—taking up Furio Jesi's expression—we might say anthropological) machine is an optical one (as is, according to the most recent studies, the apparatus described in *Leviathan*, the introduction to which perhaps provided Linnaeus with his maxim, *nosce te ipsum*, or "read thyself," as Hobbes translates this "saying not of late understood"). It is an optical machine constructed of a series of mirrors in which man, looking at himself, sees his own image always already deformed in the features of an ape. *Homo* is a constitutively "anthropomorphous" animal (that is, "resembling man," according to the term that Linnaeus constantly uses until the tenth edition of the *Systema*), who must recognize himself in a non-man in order to be human.

In medieval iconography, the ape holds a mirror in which the man who sins must recognize himself as *simia dei* {ape of God}. In Linnaeus's optical machine, whoever refuses to recognize himself in the ape, becomes one: to paraphrase Pascal, *qui fait l'homme, fait le singe* {he who acts the man, acts the ape}. This is why at the end of the introduction to the *Systema*, Linnaeus, who defined *Homo* as the animal that *is* only if it recognizes that it *is not*, must put up with apes disguised as critics climbing on his shoulders to mock him: *ideoque ringentium Satyrorum cachinnos, meisque humeris insilientium cercopithecorum exsultationes sustinui* {that is why I endured the derisive laughter of snarling satyrs and the exultation of monkeys leaping onto my shoulders}.

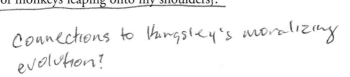

Connections to Kingsley's moralizing evolution!

§ 8   Without Rank

The anthropological machine of humanism is an ironic apparatus that verifies the absence of a nature proper to *Homo*, holding
him suspended between a celestial and a terrestrial nature,
between animal and human—and, thus, his being always less and
more than himself. This is clear in Pico's oration, that "manifesto
of humanism" that continues improperly to be called *de hominis
dignitate*, even though it does not contain the term *dignitas*, which
simply means "rank," and could not in any case refer to man. The
paradigm that it presents is anything but edifying. For the central
thesis of the oration is that man, having been molded when the
models of creation were all used up (*iam plena omnia [scil. arche-
tipa]; omnia summis, mediis infimisque ordinibus fuerant distribu-
ta*), can have neither archetype nor proper place (*certam sedem*)
nor specific rank (*nec munus ullum peculiare*).[1] Moreover, since he
was created without a definite model (*indiscretae opus imaginis*),
he does not even have a face of his own (*nec propriam faciem*)[2] and
must shape it at his own discretion in either bestial or divine form
(*tui ipsius quasi arbitrarius honorariusque plastes et fictor, in quam
malueris tute formam effingas. Poteris in inferiora quae sunt bruta
degenerare; poteris in superiora quae sunt divina ex tui animi sen-
tentia regenerari* {as the free and extraordinary maker and molder
of yourself, you may shape yourself into whatever form you prefer.
You can degenerate into the lower things, which are brutes; you

[handwritten marginalia: Kingsley's moralizing evolution?]

29

can regenerate, in accordance with your soul's decision, into the higher things, which are divine}).[3] In this definition of man by his lack of a face, the same ironic machine is at work that three centuries later will prompt Linnaeus to classify man among the *Anthropomorpha*, the "manlike" animals. Insofar as he has neither essence nor specific vocation, *Homo* is constitutively nonhuman; he can receive all natures and all faces (*Nascenti homini omnifaria semina et omnigenae vitae germina indidit Pater* {in the man being born, the Father implanted seeds of every sort and sprouts of every kind of life}),[4] and Pico can ironically emphasize his inconsistency and unclassifiability by defining him as "our chameleon" (*Quis hunc nostrum chamaeleonta non admiretur?* {who would not wonder at this chameleon of ours?}).[5] The humanist discovery of man is the discovery that he lacks himself, the discovery of his irremediable lack of *dignitas*.

To this transience and inhumanity of the human corresponds Linnaeus's registration within the species *Homo sapiens* of the enigmatic variant *Homo ferus*, a variant that seems to belie the characteristics of the most noble of the primates point for point: it is *tetrapus* (walks on all fours), *mutus* (without language), and *hirsutus* (covered with hair). The list that follows in the 1758 edition identifies this creature personally: Linnaeus is speaking of the *enfants sauvages*, or wolf-children, of whom the *Systema* records five appearances in less than fifteen years: the youth of Hannover (1724), the two *pueri pyrenaici* (1719), the *puella transisalana* (1717), and the *puella campanica* (1731). At the time when the sciences of man begin to delineate the contours of his *facies*, the *enfants sauvages*, who appear more and more often on the edges of the villages of Europe, are the messengers of man's inhumanity, the witnesses to his fragile identity and his lack of a face of his own. And when confronted with these uncertain and mute beings, the passion with which the men of the Ancien Régime try to recognize themselves in them and to "humanize" them shows how aware they are of the precariousness of the human. As Lord Monboddo writes in his preface to the English version of the *Histoire d'une jeune fille sauvage, trouvée dans les bois à l'âge de dix ans*, they knew perfectly well that "*reason* and *animal sensation*, however distinct we may imagine them, run into one another by such insensible degrees, that it is as difficult, or perhaps more difficult, to draw the line betwixt these two, than betwixt the *animal* and *vegetable*."[6] Though it will not be the case for much longer, the features of the human face are here so unsure and aleatory that they are always in the process of being undone and erased like those of a transitory being: "Who knows," writes Diderot in the *Rêve de d'Alembert*, "whether this misshapen biped a mere four feet in height, which is still called man in polar regions, but which would very soon lose that name if it went just a little more misshapen, is not the image of a passing species?"[7]

§ 9   Anthropological Machine

Homo alalus primigenius Haeckelii . . .
{Haeckel's speechless, earliest-born man . . . }

— Hans Vaihinger

In 1899 Ernst Haeckel, professor at the University of Jena, published with Kröner of Stuttgart *Die Welträtsel,* "The Enigmas of the World," which intended, against every dualism and every metaphysics, to reconcile the philosophical pursuit of truth with the advances of the natural sciences. Despite the technicality and breadth of the problems it dealt with, in a few years over 150,000 copies of the book were in print, and it became a sort of gospel of scientific progressivism. The title contains more than an ironic allusion to the lecture given by Emil Du Bois-Reymond a few years earlier at the Academy of Sciences in Berlin, in which the renowned scientist had listed seven "enigmas of the world," declaring three of them "transcendental and unsolvable," three solvable (though not yet solved), and one uncertain. In the fifth chapter of his book, Haeckel, who believes he has cleared away the first three enigmas with his own doctrine of substance, concentrates on that "problem of problems" that is the origin of man, and that in some ways encompasses Du Bois-Reymond's three solvable, though not yet solved, problems. And here too he believes he has definitively resolved the question by means of a radical and coherent application of Darwinian evolutionism.

Thomas Huxley, he explains, had already shown how the theory of "the 'descent of man from the ape' is a necessary consequence of Darwinism";[1] but it is just this certainty that imposed the difficult task of reconstructing the evolutionary history of man on the basis of both the results of comparative anatomy and the findings of paleontological research. To this task Haeckel had already, in 1874, dedicated his *Anthropogenie*, in which he reconstructed the history of man from the fish of the Silurian up through the man-apes, or Anthropomorphs, of the Miocene. But his specific contribution—of which he was rightly proud—is to have hypothesized as a form of passage from the anthropoid apes (or man-apes) to man a peculiar being that he called "ape-man" (*Affenmensch*) or, since it was without language, *Pithecanthropus alalus*:

> From the Placentals in the earliest Tertiary period (the Eocene) arise the first ancestors of the primates, the semi-apes, from which, in the Miocene, develop the true apes, and more precisely, from the Catarrhines, first come the dog-apes (the Cynopitheci) and then the man-apes (the Anthropomorphs); from one branch of the latter, during the Pliocene period, arises the ape-man without speech (the *Pithecanthropus alalus*), and from him, finally, speaking man.[2]

The existence of this pithecanthropus or ape-man, which in 1874 was merely a hypothesis, became a reality when in 1891 a Dutch military doctor, Eugen Dubois, discovered on the island of Java a piece of skull and a femur similar to those of present-day man, and, to Haeckel's great satisfaction (Dubois was an enthusiastic reader of Haeckel) baptized the being to whom they had belonged *Pithecanthropus erectus*. This, Haeckel peremptorily affirmed, "is in truth the much-sought 'missing link,' supposed to be wanting in the evolutionary chain of the primates, which stretches unbroken from the lowest Catarrhines to the highest-developed man."[3]

The idea of this *sprachloser Urmensch*—as Haeckel also defines him—entailed, however, some aporias of which he does not seem to have been aware. In reality, the passage from animal to man, despite the emphasis placed on comparative anatomy and paleontological findings, was produced by subtracting an element that had nothing to do with either one, and that instead was presupposed as the identifying characteristic of the human: language. In identifying himself with language, the speaking man places his own muteness outside of himself, as already and not yet human.

It fell to a linguist, Heymann Steinthal—who was also one of the last representatives of the *Wissenschaft des Judentums*, which had sought to apply the methods of modern science to the study of Judaism—to lay bare the aporias implicit in Haeckel's theory of the *Homo alalus* and, more generally, those of what we can call the modern anthropological machine. In his studies on the origin of language, Steinthal had himself advanced, many years before Haeckel, the idea of a prelinguistic stage of humanity. He had tried to imagine a phase of man's perceptual life in which language has not yet appeared, and he had compared this with the perceptual life of the animal; he then tried to show how language could spring from the perceptual life of man and not from that of the animal. But this is precisely where an aporia appeared which he would only fully realize some years later.

> We have [he writes] compared this purely hypothetical stage of the human soul with that of the animal, and have in the first discerned, in general and in all respects, an excess of forces. We then had the human soul apply this excess to the formation of language. We have thereby been able to show why language originated from the human soul and its perceptions, and not from that of the animal. . . . But in our description of animal and human souls we have had to leave aside language, the possibility of which we were precisely supposed to prove. It first should have been shown whence stems the force by means of which the soul forms language; this force which has the ability to create language obviously cannot stem from language. For this reason we have invented a stage of man that precedes language. But of course, this is only a fiction; for language is so necessary and natural for the human being, that without it man can neither truly exist nor be thought of as existing. Either man has language, or he simply is not. On the other hand—and this justifies the fiction—language nevertheless cannot be regarded as already inherent in the human soul; rather, it is by this time a production of man, even if not yet a fully conscious one. It is a stage of the soul's development and requires a deduction from the preceding stages. With it, true and proper human activity begins; it is the bridge that leads from the ani-

mal kingdom to the human kingdom. . . . But why the human soul alone builds this bridge, why man alone and not the animal progresses through language from animality to humanity: this is what we wanted to explain through a comparison of the animal with the animal-man. This comparison shows us that man, as we must imagine him, that is, without language, is indeed an animal-man [*Tier-Mensch*] and not a human animal [*Menschentier*], and is always already a species of man and not a species of animal.[4]

What distinguishes man from animal is language, but this is not a natural given already inherent in the psychophysical structure of man; it is, rather, a historical production which, as such, can be properly assigned neither to man nor to animal. If this element is taken away, the difference between man and animal vanishes, unless we imagine a nonspeaking *man*—*Homo alalus*, precisely—who would function as a bridge that passes from the animal to the human. But all evidence suggests that this is only a shadow cast by language, a presupposition of speaking man, by which we always obtain only an animalization of man (an animal-man, like Haeckel's ape-man) or a humanization of the animal (a man-ape). The animal-man and the man-animal are the two sides of a single fracture, which cannot be mended from either side.

Returning to his theory some years later, after having learned of Darwin's and Haeckel's theses, which by then were at the center of scientific and philosophical debates, Steinthal is perfectly well aware of the contradiction implicit in his hypothesis. What he had tried to understand was why man alone and not the animal creates language; but that was tantamount to understanding how man originates from animal. And this is precisely where the contradiction arises:

> The prelinguistic stage of intuition can only be one, not double, and it cannot be different for animal and for man. If it were different, that is, if man were naturally higher than the animal, then the origin of man would not coincide with the origin of language, but rather with the origin of his higher form of intuition out of the lower form which is the animal's. Without realizing it, I presupposed this origin: in reality, man with his human characteristics was given to me through cre-

ation, and I then sought to discover the origin of language in man. But in this way, I contradicted my presupposition: that is, that the origin of language and the origin of man were one and the same; I set man up first and then had him produce language.[5]

The contradiction that Steinthal detects here is the same one that defines the anthropological machine which—in its two variants, ancient and modern—is at work in our culture. Insofar as the production of man through the opposition man/animal, human/inhuman, is at stake here, the machine necessarily functions by means of an exclusion (which is also always already a capturing) and an inclusion (which is also always already an exclusion). Indeed, precisely because the human is already presupposed every time, the machine actually produces a kind of state of exception, a zone of indeterminacy in which the outside is nothing but the exclusion of an inside and the inside is in turn only the inclusion of an outside.

On the one hand, we have the anthropological machine of the moderns. As we have seen, it functions by excluding as not (yet) human an already human being from itself, that is, by animalizing the human, by isolating the nonhuman within the human: *Homo alalus*, or the ape-man. And it is enough to move our field of research ahead a few decades, and instead of this innocuous paleontological find we will have the Jew, that is, the non-man produced within the man, or the *néomort* and the overcomatose person, that is, the animal separated within the human body itself.

The machine of earlier times works in an exactly symmetrical way. If, in the machine of the moderns, the outside is produced through the exclusion of an inside and the inhuman produced by animalizing the human, here the inside is obtained through the inclusion of an outside, and the non-man is produced by the humanization of an animal: the man-ape, the *enfant sauvage* or *Homo ferus*, but also and above all the slave, the barbarian, and the foreigner, as figures of an animal in human form.

Both machines are able to function only by establishing a zone of indifference at their centers, within which—like a "missing link" which is always lacking because it is already virtually present—the articulation between human and animal, man and non-man, speaking being and living being, must take place. Like every space of exception, this zone is, in truth, perfectly empty, and the truly human being who should occur there is only the place of a ceaselessly updated decision in which the caesurae and their rearticulation are always dislocated and displaced anew. What would thus be obtained, however, is neither an animal life nor a human life, but only a life that is separated and excluded from itself—only a *bare life*.

And faced with this extreme figure of the human and the inhuman, it is not so much a matter of asking which of the two machines (or of the two variants of the same machine) is better or more effective—or, rather, less lethal and bloody—as it is of understanding how they work so that we might, eventually, be able to stop them.

No animal can enter into relation with an object as such.
—Jakob von Uexküll

It is fortunate that the baron Jakob von Uexküll, today considered one of the greatest zoologists of the twentieth century and among the founders of ecology, was ruined by the First World War. To be sure, even before that, as an independent researcher first in Heidelberg and then at the Zoological Station in Naples, he had earned himself a fairly good scientific reputation for his studies of the physiology and nervous system of invertebrates. But once left without his familial inheritance, he was forced to abandon the southern sun (though he kept a villa on Capri, where he would die in 1944, and where Walter Benjamin would stay for several months in 1924) and integrate himself into the University of Hamburg, founding there the Institut für Umweltforschung, which would make him famous.

Uexküll's investigations into the animal environment are contemporary with both quantum physics and the artistic avantgardes. And like them, they express the unreserved abandonment of every anthropocentric perspective in the life sciences and the radical dehumanization of the image of nature (and so it should come as no surprise that they strongly influenced both Heidegger, the philosopher of the twentieth century who more than any other strove to separate man from the living being, and Gilles Deleuze, who sought to think the animal in an absolutely nonanthropomorphic way). Where classical science saw a single world that comprised within it all living species hierarchically ordered from the most elementary forms up to the higher organisms, Uexküll instead supposes an infinite variety of perceptual worlds that, though they are uncommunicating and reciprocally exclusive, are all equally perfect and linked together as if in a gigantic musical score, at the center of which lie familiar and, at the same time, remote little beings called *Echinus esculentus, Amoeba terricola, Rhizostoma pulmo, Sipunculus, Anemonia sulcata, Ixodes ricinus,* and so on. Thus, Uexküll calls his reconstructions of the environments of the sea urchin, the amoeba, the jellyfish, the sea worm, the sea anemone, the tick (these being their common names), and the other tiny organisms of which he is particularly fond, "excursions in unknowable worlds," because these creatures' functional unity with the environment seems so apparently distant from that of man and of the so-called higher animals.

Too often, he affirms, we imagine that the relations a certain animal subject has to the things in its environment take place in the same space and in the same time as those which bind us to the objects in our human world. This illusion rests on the belief in a single world in which all living beings are situated. Uexküll shows that such a unitary world does not exist, just as a space and a time that are equal for all living things do not exist. The fly, the dragonfly, and the bee that we observe flying next to us on a sunny day do not move in the same world as the one in which we observe them, nor do they share with us—or with each other—the same time and the same space.

Uexküll begins by carefully distinguishing the *Umgebung,* the objective space in which we see a living being moving, from the *Umwelt,* the environment-world that is constituted by a more or less broad series of elements that he calls "carriers of significance" (*Bedeutungsträger*) or of "marks" (*Merkmalträger*), which are the only things that interest the animal. In reality, the *Umgebung* is our own *Umwelt,* to which Uexküll does not attribute any particular privilege and which, as such, can also vary according to the

point of view from which we observe it. There does not exist a forest as an objectively fixed environment: there exists a forest-for-
the-park-ranger, a forest-for-the-hunter, a forest-for-the-botanist,
a forest-for-the-wayfarer, a forest-for-the-nature-lover, a forest-for-
the-carpenter, and finally a fable forest in which Little Red Riding
Hood loses her way. Even a minimal detail—for example, the
stem of a wildflower—when considered as a carrier of significance,
constitutes a different element each time it is in a different environment, depending on whether, for example, it is observed in the
environment of a girl picking flowers for a bouquet to pin to her
corset, in that of an ant for whom it is an ideal way to reach its
nourishment in the flower's calyx, in that of the larva of a cicada
who pierces its medullary canal and uses it as a pump to construct
the fluid parts of its elevated cocoon, or finally in that of the cow
who simply chews and swallows it as food.

Every environment is a closed unity in itself, which results from
the selective sampling of a series of elements or "marks" in the
Umgebung, which, in turn, is nothing other than man's environment. The first task of the researcher observing an animal is to
recognize the carriers of significance which constitute its environment. These are not, however, objectively and factically isolated,
but rather constitute a close functional—or, as Uexküll prefers to
say, musical—unity with the animal's receptive organs that are
assigned to perceive the mark (*Merkorgan*) and to react to it
(*Wirkorgan*). Everything happens as if the external carrier of significance and its receiver in the animal's body constituted two elements in a single musical score, almost like two notes of the "key-
board on which nature performs the supratemporal and extraspa-
tial symphony of signification," though it is impossible to say how
two such heterogenous elements could ever have been so intimately connected.

Let us consider a spider's web from this perspective. The spider
knows nothing about the fly, nor can it measure its client as a tai-
lor does before sewing his suit. And yet it determines the length of
the stitches in its web according to the dimensions of the fly's

body, and it adjusts the resistance of the threads in exact proportion to the force of impact of the fly's body in flight. Further, the radial threads are more solid than the circular ones, because the circular threads—which, unlike the radial threads, are coated in a viscous liquid—must be elastic enough to imprison the fly and keep it from flying away. As for the radial threads, they are smooth and dry because the spider uses them as a shortcut from which to drop onto its prey and wind it finally in its invisible prison. Indeed, the most surprising fact is that the threads of the web are exactly proportioned to the visual capacity of the eye of the fly, who cannot see them and therefore flies toward death unawares. The two perceptual worlds of the fly and the spider are absolutely uncommunicating, and yet so perfectly in tune that we might say that the original score of the fly, which we can also call its original image or archetype, acts on that of the spider in such a way that the web the spider weaves can be described as "fly-like." Though the spider can in no way see the *Umwelt* of the fly (Uexküll affirms—and thus formulates a principle that would have some success—that "no animal can enter into relation with an object as such," but only with its own carriers of significance), the web expresses the paradoxical coincidence of this reciprocal blindness.

The studies by the founder of ecology follow a few years after those by Paul Vidal de la Blache on the relationship between populations and their environment (the *Tableau de la géographie de la France* is from 1903), and those of Friedrich Ratzel on the *Lebensraum*, the "vital space" of peoples (the *Politische Geographie* is from 1897), which would profoundly revolutionize human geography of the twentieth century. And it is not impossible that the central thesis of *Sein und Zeit* on being-in-the-world (*in-der-Welt-sein*) as the fundamental human structure can be read in some ways as a response to this problematic field, which at the beginning of the century essentially modified the traditional relationship between the living being and its environment-world. As is well known, Ratzel's theses, according to which all peoples are intimately linked to their vital space as their essential dimension, had a notable influence on Nazi geopolitics. This proximity is marked in a curious episode in Uexküll's intellectual biography. In 1928, five years before the advent of Nazism, this very sober scientist writes a preface to Houston Chamberlain's *Die Grundlagen des neunzehnten Jahrhunderts* {*Foundations of the Nineteeth Century*}, today considered one of the precursors of Nazism.

§ 11 Tick

The animal has memory, but no memories.

— Heymann Steinthal

Uexküll's books sometimes contain illustrations that try to suggest how a segment of the human world would appear from the point of view of a hedgehog, a bee, a fly, or a dog. The experiment is useful for the disorienting effect it produces in the reader, who is suddenly obliged to look at the most familiar places with nonhuman eyes. But never did this disorientation attain the figurative force that Uexküll was able to give to his description of the environment of the *Ixodes ricinus*, more commonly known as the tick, which certainly constitutes a high point of modern antihumanism and should be read next to *Ubu roi* and *Monsieur Teste*.

The opening has the tones of an idyll:

> Every country dweller who frequently roams the woods and bush with his dog has surely made the acquaintance of a tiny insect who, suspended from a bush's branch, waits for its prey, be it man or animal, so as to drop upon its victim and drink its blood.... Upon emerging from the egg it is not yet fully formed: it still lacks a pair of legs and the genital organs. But at this stage it is already able to attack cold-blooded animals, such as lizards, perching itself upon the tip of a blade of grass. After a few successive molts, it acquires the organs it lacked and can then set out on the hunt for warm-blooded animals.
>
> After mating, the female clambers with all her eight legs up to the tip of the protruding branch of a bush so as to be at a sufficient height either to drop upon small passing mammals or to be bumped into by larger animals.[1]

45

Following Uexküll's indications, let us try to imagine the tick suspended in her bush on a nice summer day, immersed in the sunlight and surrounded on all sides by the colors and smells of wildflowers, by the buzzing of the bees and other insects, by the birds' singing. But here, the idyll is already over, because the tick perceives absolutely none of it.

> This eyeless animal finds the way to her watchpost with the help of only her skin's general sensitivity to light. The approach of her prey becomes apparent to this blind and deaf bandit only through her sense of smell. The odor of butyric acid, which emanates from the sebaceous follicles of all mammals, works on the tick as a signal that causes her to abandon her post and fall blindly downward toward her prey. If she is fortunate enough to fall on something warm (which she perceives by means of an organ sensible to a precise temperature) then she has attained her prey, the warm-blooded animal, and thereafter needs only the help of her sense of touch to find the least hairy spot possible and embed herself up to her head in the cutaneous tissue of her prey. She can now slowly suck up a stream of warm blood.[2]

At this point, one might reasonably expect that the tick loves the taste of the blood, or that she at least possesses a sense to perceive its flavor. But it is not so. Uexküll informs us that laboratory experiments conducted using artificial membranes filled with all types of liquid show that the tick lacks absolutely all sense of taste; she eagerly absorbs any liquid that has the right temperature, that is, thirty-seven degrees centigrade, corresponding to the blood temperature of mammals. However that may be, the tick's feast of blood is also her funeral banquet, for now there is nothing left for her to do but fall to the ground, deposit her eggs and die.

The example of the tick clearly shows the general structure of the environment proper to all animals. In this particular case, the *Umwelt* is reduced to only three carriers of significance or *Merkmalträger*: (1) the odor of the butyric acid contained in the sweat of all mammals; (2) the temperature of thirty-seven degrees corresponding to that of the blood of mammals; (3) the typology of skin characteristic of mammals, generally having hair and being supplied with blood vessels. Yet the tick is immediately united to these three elements in an intense and passionate relationship the likes of which we might never find in the relations that bind man to his apparently much richer world. The tick *is* this relationship; she lives only in it and for it.

However, at this point Uexküll informs us that in the laboratory in Rostock, a tick was kept alive for eighteen years without nourishment, that is, in a condition of absolute isolation from its environment. He gives no explanation of this peculiar fact, and limits himself to supposing that in that "period of waiting" the tick lies in "a sleep-like state similar to the one we experience every night." He then draws the sole conclusion that "without a living subject, time cannot exist."[3] But what becomes of the tick and its world in this state of suspension that lasts eighteen years? How is it possible for a living being that consists entirely in its relationship with the environment to survive in absolute deprivation of that environment? And what sense does it make to speak of "waiting" without time and without world?

§ 12 Poverty in World

> The behavior of the animal is never an apprehending of
> something as something.
>
> — Martin Heidegger

In the winter semester of 1929–30, Martin Heidegger titled his
course at the University of Freiburg *Die Grundbegriffe der
Metaphysik. Welt—Endlichkeit—Einsamkeit* {*The Fundamental
Concepts of Metaphysics: World, Finitude, Solitude*}. In 1975, a year
before his death, as he was sending off the text of the course for
publication (which would happen only in 1983, as volume 29–30
of the *Gesamtausgabe*), he inscribed a dedication *in limine* to
Eugen Fink, recalling how Fink had "repeatedly expressed the wish
that this course should be published before all others." On the
author's part, it was certainly a discreet way of emphasizing the
importance that he himself must have given—and still gave—to
those lectures. On the level of theory, what justifies this chrono-
logical privilege? Why is it that these lectures should ideally pre-
cede all the others—that is, the forty-five volumes which, in the
plan of the *Gesamtausgabe*, would gather together Heidegger's
courses?

The answer is not obvious, not least because the course does
not, at first glance, correspond to its title, and in no way appears
to be an introduction to the fundamental concepts of even so spe-
cial a discipline as "first philosophy." It is dedicated first to a broad
analysis—around two hundred pages—of "profound boredom" as
a fundamental emotional tonality, and then immediately after to
an even broader inquiry into the animal's relation with its envi-

ronment and man's relation with his world.

Through the relationship between the animal's "poverty in world" (*Weltarmut*) and "world-forming" (*weltbildend*) man, Heidegger seeks to situate Dasein's fundamental structure—its being-in-the-world—with respect to the animal, and thus to inquire about the origin and sense of that openness which, with man, is produced in the living being. As is well known, Heidegger constantly rejected the traditional metaphysical definition of man as *animal rationale*, the living being that has language (or reason), as if the being of man could be determined by means of adding something to the "simply living being." Thus, in sections 10 and 12 of *Sein und Zeit*, he seeks to show how the structure of being-in-the-world that is proper to Dasein is always already presupposed in every conception (both philosophical and scientific) of life, in such a way that the latter is in truth always achieved "by way of a privative interpretation" beginning from the former.

> Life is a particular kind of being; but essentially it is accessible only in Dasein. The ontology of life is achieved only by way of a privative interpretation; it determines what must be the case if there can be anything like mere-aliveness [*Nur-noch-leben*]. Life is not a mere being-present-at-hand, nor is it Dasein. In turn, Dasein is never to be defined ontologically by regarding it as (ontologically indefinite) life plus something else.[1]

It is this metaphysical play of presupposition and reference, privation and supplement, between animal and man that the lectures of 1929–30 thematically call into question. The comparison with biology—which in *Sein und Zeit* was liquidated in a few lines—is now taken up again in the attempt to think the relation between the simply living being and Dasein in a more radical way. But this is precisely where the issue shows itself to be decisive, and the need to publish these lectures before all the others becomes clear. For in the abyss—and, at the same time, in the peculiar proximity—that the sober prose of the course opens up between animal and man, not only does *animalitas* become utterly unfamiliar and appear as "that which is most difficult to think," but *humanitas* also appears as something ungraspable and absent, suspended as it is between a "not-being-able-to-remain" and a "not-being-able-to-leave-its-place."

The guiding thread of Heidegger's exposition is constituted by the triple thesis: "the stone is worldless [*weltlos*]; the animal is poor in world [*weltarm*]; man is world-forming [*weltbildend*]." Since the stone (the nonliving being)—insofar as it lacks any possible access to what surrounds it—gets quickly set aside, Heidegger can begin his inquiry with the middle thesis, immediately taking on the problem of what it means to say "poverty in world." The philosophical analysis is here entirely oriented toward contemporary biological and zoological studies, particularly those of Hans Driesch, Karl von Baer, Johannes Müller, and above all, Müller's pupil Jakob von Uexküll. Indeed, not only are Uexküll's studies explicitly described as "the most fruitful thing that philosophy can adopt from the biology dominant today," but their influence on the concepts and terminology of the lectures is even greater than Heidegger himself recognizes when he writes that the words that he uses to define the animal's poverty in world express nothing other than what Uexküll means with the terms *Umwelt* and *Innenwelt*.[2] Heidegger gives the name *das Enthemmende*, the disinhibitor, to what Uexküll defined as the "carrier of significance" (*Bedeut-ungsträger, Merkmalträger*), and *Enthemmungsring*, disinhibiting ring, to what the zoologist called *Umwelt*, environment. Heid-egger's *Fähigsein zu*, being-capable of... , which distinguishes an organ from a simple mechanical means, corresponds to Uexküll's *Wirkorgan*. The animal is closed in the circle of its disinhibitors just as, according to Uexküll, it is closed in the few elements that define its perceptual world. For this reason, as in Uexküll, "when [the animal] comes into relation with something else, [it] can only come upon that which '*affects*' and thus starts its being-capable. Everything else is *a priori* unable to penetrate the ring around the animal."[3]

But it is in his interpretation of the animal's relationship with its disinhibiting ring and in his inquiry into the mode of being of this relation that Heidegger moves away from Uexküll to elaborate a strategy in which the understanding of "poverty in world" and the understanding of the human world proceed at an equal pace.

The mode of being proper to the animal, which defines its relation with the disinhibitor, is captivation (*Benommenheit*). Here Heidegger, with a repeated etymological figure, puts into play the relationship among the terms *benommen* (captivated, stunned, but also taken away, blocked), *eingenommen* (taken in, absorbed), and *Benehmen* (behavior), which all refer back to the verb *nehmen*, to take (from the Indo-European root **nem*, which means to distribute, to allot, to assign). Insofar as it is essentially captivated and wholly absorbed in its own disinhibitor, the animal cannot truly act (*handeln*) or comport itself (*sich verhalten*) in relation to it: it can only behave (*sich benehmen*).

> Behavior as a manner of being is in general only possible on the basis of an animal's *absorption* [Eingenommenheit] in itself. We shall define *the animal's specific being-alongside-itself*—which has nothing to do with the selfhood [*Selbstheit*] of man comporting him- or herself as a person—this absorption in itself of the animal, in which behavior of any and every kind is possible, as *captivation*. The animal can only behave insofar as it is captivated in its essence. . . . Captivation is the condition of possibility for the fact that, in accordance with its essence, the animal *behaves within an environment but never within a world* [in einer Umgebung sich benimmt, aber nie in einer Welt].[4]

For a vivid example of captivation, which can never open itself to a world, Heidegger refers to the experiment (previously described by Uexküll) in which a bee is placed in front of a cup full of honey in a laboratory. If, once it has begun to suck, the bee's abdomen is cut away, it will continue happily to suck while the honey visibly streams out of its open abdomen.

> This shows convincingly that the bee by no means recognizes the presence of too much honey. It recognizes neither this nor even—though this would be expected to touch it more closely—the absence of its abdomen. There is no question of it recognizing any of this; it continues its instinctual activity [*Treiben*] regardless, precisely because

it does not recognize that plenty of honey is still present. Rather, the bee is simply taken [*hingenommen*] by the food. This *being taken* is only possible where there is an *instinctive* "toward..." [*treibhaftes Hinzu*]. Yet this being taken in such a drivenness also excludes the possibility of any recognition of any being-present-at-hand [*Vorhandensein*]. It is precisely being taken by its food that prevents the animal from taking up a position over and against [*sich gegenüberzustellen*] this food.⁵

It is at this point that Heidegger inquires about the character of openness proper to captivation, and thus at the same time begins to carve out something like a negative image of the relationship between man and his world. To what is the bee open? What does the animal meet when it enters into relation with its disinhibitor?

Continuing to play on the compound forms of the verb *nehmen*, he writes that here we do not have an apprehending (*vernehmen*), but only an instinctive behaving (*benehmen*), insofar as the "very possibility of apprehending something as something is *withheld* [genommen] from the animal, and it is withheld from it not merely here and now, but withheld in the sense that it is 'not given at all.'"⁶ If the animal is captivated, it is because this possibility has been radically taken away from it:

> *captivation* [Benommenheit] of the animal therefore signifies: essential *withholding* [Genommenheit] *of every apprehending of something as something.* And consequently: insofar as withholding is a *being-taken* [Hingenommenheit] *by...* , the captivation of the animal characterizes the specific manner of being in which the animal relates itself to something else even while the possibility is withheld from it—or is taken away [*benommen*] from the animal, as we might also say—of comporting and relating itself to something else *as* such and such at all, *as* something present at hand, *as* a being. And it is precisely because this possibility—apprehending *as* something that to which it relates—is withheld from it that the animal can be so utterly taken by something else.⁷

After having thus introduced being into the animal's environment negatively—through its withholding—Heidegger, in some of the densest pages of the course, seeks to define more precisely the particular ontological status of that to which the animal refers in its captivation.

> Beings are *not revealed* [offenbar] to the behavior of the animal in its captivation, they are not disclosed and for that very reason are *not closed off* from it either. Captivation stands outside this possibility. We cannot say: beings are closed off from the animal. This could be the case only if there were some possibility of openness at all, however slight that might be. But the captivation of the animal places the animal essentially outside of the possibility that beings could be either disclosed to it or closed off from it. To say that captivation is the essence of animality means: *The animal as such does not stand within a potentiality for revelation* {rivelabilità, Offenbarkeit} *of beings. Neither its so-called environment nor the animal itself are revealed as beings.*[8]

The difficulty arises here from the fact that the mode of being that must be grasped is neither disclosed nor closed off, so that being in relation with it cannot properly be defined as a true relationship, as a having to do with.

> Since the animal is ceaselessly driven in its manifold instinctual activities on the basis of its captivation and of the totality of its capacities, the animal fundamentally lacks the possibility of entering into relation either with the being that it itself is or with beings other than itself. Because of this being ceaselessly driven the animal finds itself suspended, as it were, between itself and its environment, even though neither the one nor the other is experienced *as* a being. Yet this not-having any potentiality for revelation of beings, this potentiality for revelation as withheld from the animal, is at the same time a being taken by... We must say that the animal is in relation with... , that captivation and behavior display an *openness* for... For what? How are we to describe what is somehow encountered in the specific openness of being taken in the drivenness of instinctual captivation?[9]

The further definition of the ontological status of the disinhibitor leads to the heart of the thesis on poverty in world as the essential characteristic of the animal. Not being able to have-to-do-with is not purely negative: in fact, it is in some ways a form of openness, and, more precisely, an openness which nevertheless does not ever disconceal the disinhibitor as a being.

> If behavior is not a relation to beings, does this mean that it is a relation to the nothing? No! Yet if it is not a relation to the nothing, then it must be a relation to something, which surely must itself *be* and actually *is*. Certainly—but the question is precisely whether behavior is not a relation to... wherein *that to which* the behavior, as a not-having-to-do-with, relates is *open* [offen] *in a certain way* for the animal. But this certainly does not mean *disconcealed* [offenbar] *as a being*.[10]

The ontological status of the animal environment can at this point be defined: it is *offen* (open) but not *offenbar* (disconcealed; lit., openable). For the animal, beings are open but not accessible; that is to say, they are open in an inaccessibility and an opacity—that is, in some way, in a nonrelation. This *openness without disconcealment* distinguishes the animal's poverty in world from the world-forming which characterizes man. The animal is not simply without world, for insofar as it is open in captivation, it must—unlike the stone, which is worldless—do without world, lack it (*entbehren*); it can, that is, be defined in its being by a poverty and a lack:

> It is precisely because the animal in its captivation has a relation to everything encountered within its disinhibiting ring, precisely for this that it does *not* stand alongside man, precisely for this that it has *no* world. Yet this not-having of world does not force the animal alongside the stone—and does not do so for a fundamental reason. For the instinctive being-capable of taken captivation, i.e. of being taken by whatever disinhibits it, is a being open for... , even if it has the character of not-having-to-do-with... The stone on the other hand does not even have this possibility. For not-having-to-do-with... presupposes a being open. . . . The animal possesses this being-open in its essence. Being open in captivation is an *essential possession* of the animal. On the basis of this possession it can do without [*entbehren*], be poor, be determined in its being by poverty. This having is certainly *not a having of world*, but rather being taken by the disinhibiting ring—it is a *having of the disinhibitor*. But because this having is a

being-open for the disinhibitor—and yet the very possibility of having the disinhibitor revealed as a being is withheld from this being-open-for—because of this, the possession of being open is a not-having, and indeed a not having of world, if the potentiality for revelation of beings as such does indeed belong to world.[11]

§ 13   The Open

Not even the lark sees the open.

—Martin Heidegger

At stake in the course is the definition of the concept of "open" as one of the names, indeed as the name *kat' exochēn* {preeminent}, of being and of world. More than ten years later, in full world war, Heidegger returns to this concept and traces a summary genealogy of it. That it arose out of the eighth *Duino Elegy* was, in a certain sense, obvious; but in being adopted as the name of being ("the open, in which every being is freed . . . is being itself"[1]), Rilke's term undergoes an essential reversal, which Heidegger seeks to emphasize in every way. For in the eighth *Elegy* it is the animal (*die Kreatur*) that sees the open "with all its eyes," in distinct contrast to man, whose eyes have instead been "turned backward" and placed "like traps" around him. While man always has the world before him—always only stands "facing opposite" (*gegenüber*) and never enters the "pure space" of the outside—the animal instead moves in the open, in a "nowhere without the no."

This reversal of the hierarchical relationship between man and animal is precisely what Heidegger calls into question. First of all, he writes, if we think of the open as the name of what philosophy has thought of as *alētheia*, that is, as the unconcealedness-concealedness of being, then this is not truly a reversal here, because the open evoked by Rilke and the open that Heidegger's thought seeks to give back to thought have nothing in common. "For the

57

open meant by Rilke is not the open in the sense of the unconcealed. Rilke knows and suspects nothing of *alētheia*, no more
than Nietzsche does."[2] At work in both Nietzsche and Rilke is that
oblivion of being "which lies at the foundation of the biologism of
the nineteenth century and of psychoanalysis" and whose ultimate
consequence is "a monstrous anthropomorphization of . . . the
animal and a corresponding animalization of man."[3] Only man,
indeed only the essential gaze of authentic thought, can see the
open which names the unconcealedness of beings. The animal, on
the contrary, never sees this open.

> Therefore neither can an animal move about in the closed as such, no
> more than it can comport itself toward the concealed. The animal is
> excluded from the essential domain of the conflict between uncon-
> cealedness and concealedness. The sign of such an exclusion is that no
> animal or plant "has the word."[4]

At this point Heidegger, in an extremely dense page, explicitly
evokes the problem of the difference between animal environment
and human world which was at the center of the 1929–30 course:

> For the animal is in relation to his circle of food, prey, and other ani-
> mals of its own kind, and it is so in a way essentially different from
> the way the stone is related to the earth upon which it lies. In the cir-
> cle of the living things characterized as plant or animal we find the
> peculiar stirring of a motility by which the living being is "stimulat-
> ed," i.e., excited to an emerging into a circle of excitability on the
> basis of which it includes other things in the circle of its stirring. But
> no motility or excitability of plants and animals can ever bring the liv-
> ing thing into the free in such a way that what is stimulated could
> ever let the thing which excites "be" what it is even merely as excit-
> ing, not to mention what it is before the excitation and without it.
> Plant and animal depend on something outside of themselves with-
> out ever "seeing" either the outside or the inside, i.e., without ever
> seeing their being unconcealed in the free of being. It would never be
> possible for a stone, any more than for an airplane, to elevate itself
> toward the sun in jubilation and to stir like the lark, and yet not even
> the lark sees the open.[5]

The lark (this symbol, in our poetic tradition, of the purest amorous impulse—one thinks, for example, of Bernart de Ventadorn's *lauzeta*) does not see the open, because even at the moment in which it rushes toward the sun with the greatest abandon, it is blind to it; the lark can never disconceal the sun as a being, nor can it comport itself in any way toward the sun's concealedness (just like Uexküll's tick with respect to its disinhibitors). And precisely because the "essential border between the mystery of the living being (plant or animal) and the mystery of what is historical"[6] is neither experienced nor thematized in Rilke's poetry, the poetic word here falls short of a "decision capable of founding history," and is constantly exposed to the risk of "an unlimited and groundless anthropomorphization of the animal," which even places the animal above man and in a certain way makes a "super-man"[7] of it.

If the problem then is one of defining the border—at once the separation and proximity—between animal and man, perhaps the moment has come to attempt to pin down the paradoxical ontological status of the animal environment as it appears in the 1929–30 course. The animal is at once open and not open—or, better, it is neither one nor the other: it is *open in a nondisconcealment* that, on the one hand, captivates and dislocates it in its disinhibitor with unmatched vehemence, and, on the other, does not in any way disconceal as a being that thing that holds it so taken and absorbed. Heidegger seems here to oscillate between two opposite poles, which in some ways recall the paradoxes of mystical knowledge—or, rather, nonknowledge. On the one hand, captivation is a more spellbinding and intense openness than any kind of human knowledge; on the other, insofar as it is not capable of disconcealing its own disinhibitor, it is closed in a total opacity. Animal captivation and the openness of the world thus seem related to one another as are negative and positive theology, and their relationship is as ambiguous as the one which simultaneously opposes and binds in a secret complicity the dark night of the mystic and the clarity of rational knowledge. And it is perhaps to make a tacit, ironic allusion to this relationship that Heidegger feels the need at a certain point to illustrate animal captivation with one of the oldest symbols of the *unio mystica*, the moth that is burned by the flame which attracts it and yet obstinately remains unknown to the end. The symbol here shows itself to be inadequate because, according to the zoologists, what the moth is primarily blind to is precisely the non-openness of the disinhibitor, its own remaining captivated by it. While mystical knowledge is essentially the experience of a nonknowledge and of a concealment as such, the animal cannot comport itself toward the not open; it remains excluded precisely from the essential domain of the conflict between disconcealment and concealment.

Nevertheless, in Heidegger's course the animal's poverty in world is at times reversed into an incomparable wealth, and the thesis according to which the animal is lacking in world is called into question as an undue projection of the human world onto the animal.

> The difficulty of the problem lies in the fact that in our questioning we must always interpret the poverty in world and the peculiar encirclement of the animal in such a way that we end up talking as if that to which the animal relates . . . were a being, and as if the relation were an ontological relation that is manifest to the animal. The fact that this is not the case compels us to the thesis that the *essence of life is accessible only through a destructive observation,* which does not mean that life is something inferior or that it is at a lower level in comparison with human Dasein. On the contrary, life is a domain which possesses a wealth of being-open, of which the human world may know nothing at all.[8]

But then, when it appears that the thesis must be unreservedly abandoned, and animal environment and human world seem to diverge into a radical heterogeneity, Heidegger proposes it once again through a reference to the famous passage in the Letter to the Romans 8:19, in which Paul evokes the creature's yearning expectation for redemption, so that the animal's poverty in world now appears to reflect "a problem internal to animality itself":

We must, then, *leave open the possibility* that the authentic and explicitly metaphysical understanding of the essence of world compels us to understand the animal's not-having of world as a *doing-without after all*, and to find a *being-poor* in the manner of being of the animal as such. The fact that biology recognizes nothing of the sort is no counter-argument against metaphysics. That perhaps only poets occasionally speak of this is an argument that metaphysics cannot be allowed to cast to the winds. In the end the Christian faith is not necessary in order to understand something of the word which Paul (Romans 8:19) writes concerning the *apokaradokia tēs ktiseōs*, the yearning expectation of creatures and creation, the paths of which, as the Fourth Book of Ezra 7:12 says, have become narrow, doleful, and tiresome in this aeon. But nor is any pessimism required in order to develop the *animal's poverty in world as a problem internal to animality itself*. For with the animal's being open for that which disinhibits, the animal in its captivation is essentially held out in something other than itself, something that indeed cannot be manifest to the animal either as a being or as a non-being, but which, insofar as it disinhibits . . . brings an *essential disruption* [wesenhafte Erschütterung] into the essence of the animal.[9]

As the *apokaradokia* suddenly brought the creature closer to man in the Pauline Letter's perspective of messianic redemption, so too the essential disruption that the animal experiences in its being exposed in a nondisconcealment drastically shortens the distance that the course had marked out between animal and man, between openness and non-openness. That is to say that poverty in world—in which the animal in some way feels its own not-being-open—has the strategic function of ensuring a passage between the animal environment and the open, from a perspective in which captivation as the essence of the animal is "as it were a suitable background against which the essence of humanity can now be set off."[10]
At this point Heidegger can return to the discussion of boredom that had occupied him in the first part of the course, and can put animal captivation and the fundamental *Stimmung* that he had called "profound boredom" (*tiefe Langeweile*) in unexpected resonance with each other:

It will be seen how this fundamental attunement,[11] and everything bound up with it, is to be set off over against what we claimed as the essence of animality, over against captivation. This contrast will become all the more decisive for us insofar as captivation, as precisely the essence of animality, apparently finds itself in the closest proximity to what we identified as a characteristic element of profound boredom and described as the *enchantment-enchainment* [Gebanntheit] of Dasein within beings in their totality. Certainly it will be seen that this closest proximity of both essential constitutions is merely deceptive, and that an abyss lies between them which cannot be bridged by any mediation whatsoever. Yet in that case the total divergence of these two theses will suddenly become very clear to us, and thereby the essence of world.[12]

Captivation appears here as a sort of fundamental *Stimmung* in which the animal does not open itself, as does Dasein, in a world, yet is nevertheless ecstatically drawn outside of itself in an exposure which disrupts it in its every fiber. And the understanding of the human world is possible only through the experience of the "closest proximity"—even if deceptive—to this *exposure without disconcealment.* Perhaps it is not the case that being and the human world have been presupposed in order then to reach the animal by means of subtraction—that is, by a "destructive observation"; perhaps the contrary is also, and even more, true, that is, that the openness of the human world (insofar as it is also and primarily an openness to the essential conflict between disconcealment and concealment) can be achieved only by means of an operation enacted upon the not-open of the animal world. And the place of this operation—in which human openness in a world and animal openness toward its disinhibitor seem for a moment to meet—is boredom.

§ 14   Profound Boredom

> Boredom is the desire for happiness left in its pure state.
>
> — Giacomo Leopardi

The discussion of boredom occupies sections 18–39 (nearly one hundred and eighty pages) of the course and thus constitutes the broadest analysis Heidegger ever dedicated to a *Stimmung* (in *Sein und Zeit* the discussion of anxiety takes up only eight pages). After having raised the problem of how something like an attunement—that is, the fundamental manner in which Dasein is always already predisposed, and thus the most originary way in which we encounter ourselves and others—must be understood in general, Heidegger articulates his analysis by following the three forms or degrees through which boredom progressively intensifies until it reaches the figure that he defines as "profound boredom" (*tiefe Langeweile*). These three forms converge in two characteristics or "structural moments" (*Strukturmomente*) that, according to Heidegger, define the essence of boredom. The first is *Leergelassenheit*, being-left-empty, abandonment in emptiness. Heidegger begins with a description of what must have appeared to his eyes as a sort of *locus classicus* of the experience of boredom.

> We are sitting, for example, at the tasteless station of some lonely minor railway. It is four hours until the next train arrives. The district is unattractive. We do have a book in our rucksack, though—shall we read? No. Or think through a problem, some question? We are unable to. We read the timetables or study the table giving the various distances from this station to other places we are not otherwise acquaint-

ed with at all. We look at the clock—only a quarter of an hour has gone by. Then we go out onto the main road. We walk up and down, just to have something to do. But it is no use. Then we count the trees along the main road, look at our watch again—exactly five minutes since we last looked at it. Fed up with walking back and forth, we sit down on a stone, draw all kinds of figures in the sand, and in doing so catch ourselves looking at our watch yet again—half an hour—and so on.[1]

The diversions with which we try to occupy ourselves bear witness to being-left-empty as the essential experience of boredom. While we are usually constantly occupied with and in things (indeed, Heidegger states this more precisely in terms that anticipate those which will define the animal's relationship with its environment: "we are *taken* [hingenommen] by things, if not altogether *lost* in them, and often even *captivated* [benommen] by them"[2]), in boredom we suddenly find ourselves abandoned in emptiness. But in this emptiness, things are not simply "carried away from us or annihilated";[3] they are there, but "they have nothing to offer us"; they leave us completely indifferent, yet in such a way that we cannot free ourselves from them, because *we are riveted and delivered over to what bores us*: "In becoming bored by something we are precisely still held fast [festgehalten] by that which is boring, we do not yet let it go [*wir lassen es selbst noch nicht los*], or we are compelled by it, bound to it for whatever reason."[4]

And this is where boredom is revealed to be something like the fundamental and properly constitutive *Stimmung* of Dasein, compared to which the anxiety of *Sein und Zeit* seems merely to be a sort of answer or reactive response. For in indifference

beings in their totality do not disappear, but rather *show themselves as such precisely* in their indifference. The *emptiness* accordingly here consists in the *indifference* enveloping beings *in their totality*. . . . This means that Dasein finds itself set in place by boredom precisely before beings in their totality, to the extent that in this form of boredom the beings that surround us offer us no further possibility of action and no further possibility of our letting anything act. They refuse themselves in their totality [*es versagt sich im Ganzen*] in relation to these possibilities. They refuse themselves to a Dasein that, as such, in the midst of these beings in their totality, comports itself toward them—toward them, toward those beings in their totality that now refuse themselves—and must comport itself toward them, if it is indeed to be what it is. Dasein thus finds itself delivered over to beings that refuse themselves in their totality [*Das Dasein findet sich so ausgeliefert an das sich im Ganzen versagende Seiende*].[5]

In this being "delivered over to beings that refuse themselves" as the first essential moment of boredom, the constitutive structure of that being—Dasein, for whom, in its being, its very being is at stake—is thus revealed. In boredom, Dasein can be riveted to beings that refuse themselves in their totality because it is constitutively "delivered up [*überantwortet*] to its own proper being," factically "thrown" and "lost" in the world of its concern. But, precisely for this reason, boredom brings to light the unexpected proximity of Dasein and the animal. *In becoming bored, Dasein is delivered over (*ausgeliefert*) to something that refuses itself, exactly as the animal, in its captivation, is exposed (*hinausgesetzt*) in something unrevealed.*

In being left empty by profound boredom, something vibrates like an echo of that "essential disruption" that arises in the animal from its being exposed and taken in an "other" that is, however, never revealed to it as such. For this reason the man who becomes bored finds himself in the "closest proximity"—even if it is only apparent—to animal captivation. Both are, in their most proper gesture, *open to a closedness*; they are totally delivered over to something that obstinately refuses itself (and, if we may attempt to identify something like the characteristic *Stimmung* of every thinker, perhaps it is precisely this being delivered over to something that refuses itself that defines the specific emotional tonality of Heidegger's thought).

The analysis of the second "structural moment" of profound boredom allows us to clarify both its proximity to animal captivation and the step which boredom takes beyond it. This second structural moment (which is closely tied to the first, being-left-empty) is being-held-in-suspense (*Hingehaltenheit*). For beings' refusal of themselves in their totality, which took place in the first moment, in some ways makes what Dasein could have done or experienced—that is to say, its possibilities—manifest by means of a withholding. These possibilities now stand before Dasein in their absolute indifference, both present and perfectly inaccessible at the same time:

> This refusal tells of these possibilities of Dasein. This refusal does not speak about them, does not open a discussion about them, but in its refusal it *points to them* and makes them known in refusing them. . . . Beings in their totality have become indifferent. Yet not only that, but simultaneously something else shows itself: there occurs the dawning of the possibilities that Dasein could have, but which lie inactive [*brachliegende*] precisely in this "it is boring for one," and as unutilized leave us in the lurch. In any case, we see that in refusal there lies a reference to something else. This reference is the *announcement of the possibilities which lie inactive.*[6]

The verb *brachliegen*—which we have translated as "to lie inactive"—comes from the language of agriculture. *Brache* means "fallow ground," that is, the field that is left unworked in order to be planted the following year. *Brachliegen* means "to leave fallow," that is, inactive, uncultivated. And in this way, the meaning of being-held-in-suspense as the second structural moment of profound boredom is also revealed. Now it is the specific possibilities of Dasein, its potentiality for doing {*poter fare*} this or that, which are being held in suspense and lie inactive. But this deactivation of the concrete possibilities makes manifest for the first time what generally *makes* pure possibility *possible* (*das Ermöglichende*)—or, as Heidegger says, "the originary *possibilitization*" (*die ursprüngliche* Ermöglichung):

> Dasein as such—i.e., whatever belongs to its potentiality for being as such, whatever concerns the possibility of Dasein as such—is at issue in beings that refuse themselves in their totality. What concerns a possibility as such, however, is whatever *makes it possible*, that which lends it possib*ility* as this very thing which is possible. Whatever is

utmost and primary in making possible all possibilities of Dasein as possibilities, whatever it is that bears Dasein's potentiality for being, its possibilities, is at issue in beings that refuse themselves in their totality. This means, however, that those beings refusing themselves in their totality do not make an announcement concerning arbitrary possibilities of myself, they do not report on them, rather insofar as this announcement in refusal is a *calling* [Anrufen], it is that which makes authentically possible the Dasein in me. This calling of possibilities as such, which goes together with the refusal, is not some indeterminate pointing to [*Hinweisen*] arbitrary, changing possibilities of Dasein, but an utterly unequivocal pointing to *whatever it is* that make possible, bears and guides all essential possibilities of Dasein, for which we apparently have no content, so that we cannot say what it is in the same way that we point out things present at hand and determine them as this or that. . . . This announcing pointing toward that which makes Dasein authentically possible in its possibilities is a *necessary compulsion* [Hinzwingen] *toward the singular extremity of this originary making possible.* . . . To this coming to be left in the lurch by beings which refuse themselves in their totality there simultaneously belongs our being-compelled toward this utmost extremity of the possibilitization proper to Dasein as such.[7]

Being-held-in-suspense as the second essential characteristic of profound boredom, then, is nothing but this experience of the disconcealing of the originary possibilitization (that is, pure potentiality) in the suspension and withholding of all concrete and specific possibilities.

What appears for the first time as such in the deactivation (in the *Brachliegen*) of possibility, then, is the *very origin of potentiality*—and with it, of Dasein, that is, the being which exists in the form of potentiality-for-being {*poter-essere*}. But precisely for this reason, this potentiality or originary possibilitization constitutively has the form of a potential-not-to {*potenza-di-no*}, of an impotentiality, insofar as it is *able to* {può} only in beginning from a *being able not to* {poter non}, that is, from a deactivation of single, specific, factical possibilities.

Thus, the proximity, and at the same time the distance, between profound boredom and animal captivation finally come to light.

In captivation the animal was in an immediate relation with its disinhibitor, exposed to and stunned by it, yet in such a way that the disinhibitor could never be revealed as such. What the animal is precisely unable to do is suspend and deactivate its relationship with the ring of its specific disinhibitors. The animal environment is constituted in such a way that something like a pure possibility can never become manifest within it. Profound boredom then appears as the metaphysical operator in which the passage from poverty in world to world, from animal environment to human world, is realized; at issue here is nothing less than anthropogenesis, the becoming Da-sein of living man. But this passage, this *becoming*-Dasein of living man (or, as Heidegger also writes in the course, this taking on of the burden which, for man, is Dasein), does not open onto a further, wider, and brighter space, achieved beyond the limits of the animal environment, and unrelated to it; on the contrary, it is opened only by means of a suspension and a deactivation of the animal relation with the disinhibitor. In this suspension, in this remaining-inactive (*brachliegend,* lying fallow) of the disinhibitor, the animal's captivation and its being exposed in something unrevealed can for the first time be grasped as such. The open and the free-of-being do not name something radically other with respect to the neither-open-nor-closed of the animal environment: they are the appearing of an undisconcealed as such, the suspension and capture of the lark-not-seeing-the-open. The jewel set at the center of the human world and its *Lichtung* {clearing} is nothing but animal captivation; the wonder "that beings *are*" is nothing but the grasping of the "essential disruption" that occurs in the living being from its being exposed in a nonrevelation. In this sense, the *Lichtung* truly is a *lucus a non lucendo*: the openness at stake in it is essentially the openness to a closedness, and whoever looks in the open sees only a closing, only a not-seeing.

In his course on Parmenides, Heidegger insists several times on the primacy of *lēthē* with respect to unconcealedness. The origin of concealedness (*Verborgenheit*) with respect to unconcealedness (*Unverborgenheit*) remains so much in the shadows that it could in some ways be defined as the originary secret of unconcealedness: "On the one hand, the word 'un-concealedness' directs us to something like 'concealedness.' What, as regards 'un-concealedness,' is previously concealed, who does the concealing and how it takes place, when and where and for whom concealment exists, all that remains undetermined."[8] "Where there is concealedness, a concealing must occur or must have occurred. . . . But what it is the Greeks experience and think when they allude to a concealedness in every 'unconcealedness' is not immediately clear."[9] From the perspective that we have tried to sketch out, this secret of unconcealedness must be unraveled in this sense: the *lēthē* that holds sway at the center of *alētheia*—the nontruth that also belongs originarily to the truth—is undisconcealedness {*indisvelatezza*}, the not-open of the animal. The irresolvable struggle between unconcealedness and concealedness, between disconcealment and concealment, which defines the human world, is the internal struggle between man and animal.

For this reason, the belonging to each other of being and nothingness is at the center of the lecture "Was ist Metaphysik?," which was delivered in July 1929—and is thus contemporary with the preparation of the course on the *Grundbegriffe der Metaphysik*. "Da-sein means: being held suspended in the nothing [*Hineingehaltenheit*, nearly the same word that describes the second essential characteristic of boredom]."[10] "Human Dasein can comport itself [*verhalten*, the term that, in the course, defines the human relationship with the world in opposition to the *sichbenehmen* of the animal] toward beings only if it holds itself suspended in the nothing."[11] The *Stimmung* of anxiety appears in the lecture (where boredom is not mentioned) as the taking on of that originary openness which is produced only in the "clear night of the nothing."[12] But where does this negativity that nihilates (*nichtet*) in being itself come from? A comparison of the lecture and the course of the same period suggests some possible answers to this question.

From the beginning, being is traversed by the nothing; the *Lichtung* is also originarily *Nichtung*, because the world has become open for man only through the interruption and nihilation of the living being's relationship with its disinhibitor. To be sure, just as the living being does not know being, neither does it know the nothing; but being appears in the "clear night of the nothing" only because man, in the experience of profound boredom, has risked himself in the suspension of his relationship with the environment as a living being. *Lēthē*—which, according to the introduction to the lecture, is what reigns in the open as *das Wesende*, what essences {*essentifica*} and gives being, while remaining unthought in it—is nothing but the undisconcealed of the animal environment, and to remember the one necessarily means to remember the other, to remember captivation an instant before a world disclosed itself. What essences and, at the same time, nihilates in being, arises out of the animal disinhibitor's being "neither a being nor a non-being." Dasein is simply an animal that has learned to become bored; it has awakened *from* its own captivation *to* its own captivation. This awakening of the living being to its own being-captivated, this anxious and resolute opening to a not-open, is the human.

In 1929, while preparing his course, Heidegger could not have known the description of the tick's world, which is not in the texts to which he refers, and is introduced by Uexküll only in 1934, in his book *Streifzüge durch die Umwelten von Tieren und Menschen.* Had he known it, he would perhaps have inquired about the eighteen years the tick survived in the Rostock laboratory in the absolute absence of its disinhibitors. Under particular circumstances, like those which man creates in laboratories, the animal can effectively suspend its immediate relationship with its environment, without, however, either ceasing to be an animal or becoming human. Perhaps the tick in the Rostock laboratory guards a mystery of the "simply living being," which neither Uexküll nor Heidegger was prepared to confront.

§ 15 World and Earth

The relation between man and animal, between world and environment, seems to evoke that intimate strife (*Streit*) between world and earth which, according to Heidegger, is at issue in the work of art. In both cases, there seems to be present a single paradigm which presses together an openness and a closedness. For similarly at issue in the work of art—in the conflict between world and earth—is a dialectic between concealedness and unconcealedness, openness and closedness, which Heidegger in his essay "Der Ursprung des Kunstwerkes" evokes in nearly the same terms as those of the 1929–30 course: "The stone is worldless. Plant and animal likewise have no world; but they belong to the veiled throng of an environment in which they hang suspended. The peasant woman, on the other hand, has a world because she dwells in the open of beings."[1] If in the work the world represents the open, then the earth names "that which essentially closes itself in itself."[2] "The earth appears only where it is guarded and preserved as the essentially Undisclosable, which withdraws from every opening and constantly keeps itself closed."[3] In the work of art, this Undisclosable comes to light as such. "The work moves the earth itself into the open of a world and keeps it there."[4] "To produce the earth means: to bring it into the open as that which closes itself in itself {*In-sé-chiudentesi, Sichverschließende*}."[5]

World and earth, openness and closedness—though opposed in

an essential conflict—are, however, never separable: "The earth is the spontaneous emerging toward nothing of that which constantly closes itself and thus saves itself. World and earth are essentially different from one another and yet are never separated. The world grounds itself on the earth, and earth juts through world."[6]

It is not surprising that Heidegger describes this inseparable opposition of world and earth in terms that appear to have a decidedly political coloration.

> The reciprocal opposition of world and earth is strife [*Streit*]. But we would surely all too easily misunderstand the essence of the strife if we were to confound it with discord and dispute, and thus see it only as disturbance and destruction. In essential strife, rather, the opponents raise each other into the self-assertion [*Selbstbehauptung*] of their essence. The self-assertion of essence, however, is never a rigid insistence upon some contingent state, but surrender to the concealed originality of the provenance of one's own being. . . . The more strife overdoes itself and asserts itself, the more intransigently do the opponents let themselves go into the intimacy of simple belonging to one another. The earth cannot do without the open of the world if it itself is to appear as earth in the liberated throng of its closing itself. The world in turn cannot soar away from the earth if, as the governing breadth and path of every essential historical destiny, it is to ground itself on a resolute foundation.[7]

It is beyond question that for Heidegger a political paradigm (indeed the political paradigm par excellence) is at stake in the dialectic between concealedness and unconcealedness. In the course on Parmenides, the *polis* is defined precisely by the conflict between *Verborgenheit* and *Unverborgenheit*.

> The *polis* is the place, gathered into itself, of the unconcealedness of beings. If now, however, as the word indicates, *alētheia* possesses a conflictual essence, and if this conflictuality appears also in the relation of opposition to distortion and oblivion, then in the *polis* as the essential place of man there has to hold sway every extreme opposition, and therein every in-essence, to the unconcealed and to beings, i.e., non-beings in the multiplicity of their counter-essences.[8]

The ontological paradigm of truth as the conflict between concealedness and unconcealedness is, in Heidegger, immediately and originarily a political paradigm. It is because man essentially occurs in the openness to a closedness that something like a *polis* and a politics are possible.

If we now, following the interpretation of the 1929–30 course that we have been suggesting, restore to the closed, to the earth, and to *lēthē* their proper name of "animal" and "simply living being," then the originary political conflict between unconcealedness and concealedness will be, at the same time and to the same degree, that between the humanity and the animality of man. The animal is the Undisclosable which man keeps and brings to light as such. But here everything becomes complicated. For if what is proper to *humanitas* is to remain open to the closedness of the animal, if what the world brings into the open is precisely and only the earth as what closes itself in itself, then how must we understand Heidegger's reproach of metaphysics, and of the sciences that depend on it, for their thinking man "beginning with his *animalitas* and not [thinking] in the direction of his *humanitas*"?[9] If humanity has been obtained only through a suspension of animality, and must thus keep itself open to the closedness of animality, in what sense does Heidegger's attempt to grasp the "existing essence of man" escape the metaphysical primacy of *animalitas*?

§ 16   Animalization

Men are animals, some of whom raise their own kind.

—Peter Sloterdijk

Heidegger was perhaps the last philosopher to believe in good faith that the place of the *polis* (the *polos* {pole} where the conflict between concealedness and unconcealedness, between the *animalitas* and the *humanitas* of man, reigns) was still practicable, and that it was still possible for men, for a people—holding themselves in that risky place—to find their own proper historical destiny. He was, that is, the last to believe (at least up to a certain point, and not without doubts and contradictions) that the anthropological machine, which each time decides upon and recomposes the conflict between man and animal, between the open and the not-open, could still produce history and destiny for a people. It is likely that at a certain point he realized his error, and understood that a decision that responded to a historical mission of being was nowhere possible. Already in 1934–35, in the course on Hölderlin in which he attempts to reawaken the "fundamental emotional tonality of Dasein's historicity," he writes that "the possibility of a great disruption [*Erschütterung*, the same term that describes the animal's being exposed in something undisconcealed] of historical existence of a people has disappeared. Temples, images, and customs are no longer capable of taking on the historical vocation of a people in order to compel it in a new task."[1] By this point, post-history was beginning to knock on the doors of a concluded metaphysics.

75

Today, at a distance of nearly seventy years, it is clear for anyone
who is not in absolutely bad faith that there are no longer historical tasks that can be taken on by, or even simply assigned to, men.
It was in some ways already evident starting with the end of the
First World War that the European nation-states were no longer
capable of taking on historical tasks and that peoples themselves
were bound to disappear. We completely misunderstand the
nature of the great totalitarian experiments of the twentieth century if we see them only as a carrying out of the nineteenth-cen-
tury nation-states' last great tasks: nationalism and imperialism.
The stakes are now different and much higher, for it is a question
of taking on as a task the very factical existence of peoples, that is,
in the last analysis, their bare life. Seen in this light, the totalitar-
ianisms of the twentieth century truly constitute the other face of
the Hegelo-Kojevian idea of the end of history: man has now
reached his historical *telos* and, for a humanity that has become
animal again, there is nothing left but the depoliticization of
human societies by means of the unconditioned unfolding of the
oikonomia, or the taking on of biological life itself as the supreme
political (or rather impolitical) task.

It is likely that the times in which we live have not emerged
from this aporia. Do we not see around and among us men and
peoples who no longer have any essence or identity—who are
delivered over, so to speak, to their inessentiality and their inactivity {*inoperosità*}—and who grope everywhere, and at the cost of
gross falsifications, for an inheritance and a task, *an inheritance as
task*? Even the pure and simple relinquishment of all historical
tasks (reduced to simple functions of internal or international
policing) in the name of the triumph of the economy, often today
takes on an emphasis in which natural life itself and its well-being
seem to appear as humanity's last historical task—if indeed it
makes sense here to speak of a "task."

The traditional historical potentialities—poetry, religion, philosophy—which from both the Hegelo-Kojevian and Heidegger-
ian perspectives kept the historico-political destiny of peoples
awake, have long since been transformed into cultural spectacles

and private experiences, and have lost all historical efficacy. Faced with this eclipse, the only task that still seems to retain some seriousness is the assumption of the burden—and the "total management"—of biological life, that is, of the very animality of man. Genome, global economy, and humanitarian ideology are the three united faces of this process in which posthistorical humanity seems to take on its own physiology as its last, impolitical mandate.

It is not easy to say whether the humanity that has taken upon itself the mandate of the total management of its own animality is still human, in the sense of that *humanitas* which the anthropological machine produced by de-ciding every time between man and animal; nor is it clear whether the well-being of a life that can no longer be recognized as either human or animal can be felt as fulfilling. To be sure, such a humanity, from Heidegger's perspective, no longer has the form of keeping itself open to the undisconcealed of the animal, but seeks rather to open and secure the not-open in every domain, and thus closes itself to its own openness, forgets its *humanitas*, and makes being its specific disinhibitor. The total humanization of the animal coincides with a total animalization of man.

§ 17   Anthropogenesis

Let us try to state the provisional results of our reading of Western philosophy's anthropological machine in the form of theses:

1. Anthropogenesis is what results from the caesura and articulation between human and animal. This caesura passes first of all within man.

2. Ontology, or first philosophy, is not an innocuous academic discipline, but in every sense the fundamental operation in which anthropogenesis, the becoming human of the living being, is realized. From the beginning, metaphysics is taken up in this strategy: it concerns precisely that *meta* that completes and preserves the overcoming of animal *physis* in the direction of human history. This overcoming is not an event that has been completed once and for all, but an occurrence that is always under way, that every time and in each individual decides between the human and the animal, between nature and history, between life and death.

3. Being, world, and the open are not, however, something other with respect to animal environment and life: they are nothing but the interruption and capture of the living being's relationship with its disinhibitor. The open is nothing but a grasping of the animal not-open. Man suspends his animality and, in this way, opens a "free and empty" zone in which life is captured and a-bandoned {*ab-bandonata*} in a zone of exception.

4. Precisely because the world has been opened for man only by means of the suspension and capture of animal life, being is always already traversed by the nothing; the *Lichtung* is always already *Nichtung*.

5. In our culture, the decisive political conflict, which governs every other conflict, is that between the animality and the humanity of man. That is to say, in its origin Western politics is also biopolitics.

6. If the anthropological machine was the motor for man's becoming historical, then the end of philosophy and the completion of the epochal destinations of being mean that today the machine is idling.

At this point, two scenarios are possible from Heidegger's perspective: (*a*) posthistorical man no longer preserves his own animality as undisclosable, but rather seeks to take it on and govern it by means of technology; (*b*) man, the shepherd of being, appropriates his own concealedness, his own animality, which neither remains hidden nor is made an object of mastery, but is thought as such, as pure abandonment.

biopower

§ 18 Between

All the enigmas of the world seem slight to us compared to the tiny secret of sex.

— Michel Foucault

Several of Benjamin's texts propose an entirely different image of the relationship between man and nature and between nature and history: an image in which the anthropological machine seems to be completely out of play. The first is the letter of December 9, 1923, to Rang on the "saved night." Here nature, as the world of closedness (*Verschlossenheit*) and of the night, is opposed to history as the sphere of revelation (*Offenbarung*). But to the closed sphere of nature Benjamin—surprisingly—also ascribes ideas as well as works of art. Indeed, these last are defined

> as models of a nature that awaits no day, and thus no Judgement Day;
> they are the models of a nature that is neither the theater of history
> nor the dwelling place of man. The saved night [*Die gerettete Nacht*].[1]

The link that Paul's text on the *apokaradokia tēs ktiseōs* established between nature and redemption, between creature and redeemed humanity, is here shattered. Ideas—which, like stars, "shine only in the night of nature"—gather creatural life not in order to reveal it, nor to open it to human language, but rather to give it back to its closedness and muteness. The separation between nature and redemption is an ancient Gnostic motif; and this led Jacob Taubes to place Benjamin alongside the Gnostic Marcion. But in Benjamin, the separation follows a peculiar strategy, one that is at antipodes with Marcion's. What in Marcion, as in the majority of the Gnostics, arose out of an undervaluation and condemnation of nature as the work of the bad Demiurge, here leads instead to a transvaluation which sets it up as the archetype of *beatitudo*. The "saved night" is the name of this nature that has been given back to itself, whose character, according to another of Benjamin's fragments, is transience and whose rhythm is beatitude. The salvation that is at issue here does not concern something that has been lost and must be found again, something that has been forgotten and must be remembered; it concerns, rather, the lost and the forgotten as such—that is, something unsavable. The saved night is a relationship with something unsavable. For this reason, man—insofar as he is "at some stages" also nature—appears as a field traversed by two distinct tensions, by two different redemptions:

> To the spiritual *restitutio in integrum*, which introduces immortality, corresponds a worldly restitution that leads to the eternity of a downfall, and the rhythm of this worldly existence which eternally passes away—passes away in its totality, in its spatial but also in its temporal totality—the rhythm of messianic nature, is happiness.[2]

In this singular gnosis, man is the sieve in which creatural life and spirit, creation and redemption, nature and history are continually discerned and separated, yet nevertheless continue to conspire toward their own salvation.

In the text that concludes *Einbahnstraße* and bears the heading *Zum Planetarium*, Benjamin seeks to outline modern man's relationship with nature as compared to ancient man's relationship with the cosmos, which had its place in the ecstatic trance. For modern man the proper place of this relationship is technology. But not, to be sure, a technology conceived, as it commonly is, as man's mastery of nature:

> The mastery of nature (so the imperialists teach) is the sense of all technology. But who would trust a cane wielder who proclaimed the mastery of children by adults to be the sense of education? Is not edu-

cation, above all, the indispensable ordering of the relationship between generations and therefore mastery (if we are to use this term) of that relationship and not of children? And likewise technology is the mastery not of nature but mastery of the relation between nature and humanity. It is true that men as a species completed their evolution thousands of years ago; but humanity as a species is just beginning its.[3]

What does "mastery of the relation between nature and humanity" mean? That neither must man master nature nor nature man. Nor must both be surpassed in a third term that would represent their dialectical synthesis. Rather, according to the Benjaminian model of a "dialectic at a standstill," what is decisive here is only the "between," the interval or, we might say, the play between the two terms, their immediate constellation in a non-coincidence. The anthropological machine no longer articulates nature and man in order to produce the human through the suspension and capture of the inhuman. The machine is, so to speak, stopped; it is "at a standstill," and, in the reciprocal suspension of the two terms, something for which we perhaps have no name and which is neither animal nor man settles in between nature and humanity and holds itself in the mastered relation, in the saved night.

A few pages earlier in the same book, in one of his densest aphorisms, Benjamin evokes the uncertain image of this life that has freed itself from its relation with nature only at the cost of losing its own mystery. What severs—not solves—this secret bond that ties man to life, however, is an element which seems to belong totally to nature but instead everywhere surpasses it: sexual fulfillment. In the paradoxical image of a life that, in the extreme vicissitude of sensual pleasure, frees itself of its mystery in order to, so to speak, recognize a nonnature, Benjamin has set down something like the hieroglyph of a new in-humanity:

> Sexual fulfillment delivers the man from his mystery, which does not consist in sexuality but which in its fulfillment, and perhaps in it alone, is severed—not solved. It is comparable to the fetters that bind

him to life. The woman cuts them, and the man is free to die because his life has lost its mystery. Thereby he is reborn, and as his beloved frees him from the mother's spell, the woman literally detaches him from Mother Earth—a midwife who cuts that umbilical cord which the mystery of nature has woven.[4]

§ 19   *Desœuvrement*

In the Kunsthistorisches Museum of Vienna there is a late work by Titian (defined by some, indeed, as his *ultima poesia*, something of a farewell to painting) known as the *Nymph and Shepherd*. The two figures are represented in the foreground, immersed in a dark country landscape; the shepherd, seated facing us, holds a flute in his hands as if he had just taken it from his lips. The nymph, nude and represented from the back, lies stretched next to him on a leopard's skin, a traditional symbol for wantonness and libido, showing her full and luminous hips. With a studied gesture, she turns her pensive face toward the viewers, and with her left hand lightly touches her other arm in a sort of caress. A little further in the distance, there is a tree that has been struck by lightning, half dry and half green, like the tree in the allegory of Lot, against which an animal—a "bold goat" according to some, but perhaps a fawn—dramatically rears up, as if to nibble at its leaves. Still higher, as is often the case in the late, impressionist Titian, one's gaze becomes lost in a vivid mass of painting.

Faced with this enigmatic *paysage moralisé* immersed in an atmosphere of both exhausted sensuality and subdued melancholy, scholars have been left perplexed, and no explanation has seemed complete. To be sure, the scene is "too much fraught with emotion to be an allegory," and yet "this emotion is too restrained and somber for any of the suggestions proposed."[1] It seems obvi-

ous that the nymph and the shepherd are linked erotically; but
their relationship, at once promiscuous and remote, is so peculiar
that they must be "despondent lovers, so near to each other in
body yet so far apart in sentiment."[2] And everything in the painting—the nearly monochromatic tone of the colors, the dark and
brooding expression of the woman, as well as her pose—"suggests
that this couple have eaten from the Tree of Knowledge and that
they are losing their Eden."[3]

The relation of this painting to another by Titian, *The Three
Ages of Man*, in the National Gallery of Scotland in Edinburgh,
has been rightly observed by Judith Dundas. According to the
scholar, the painting in Vienna—done many years later—takes up
several of the elements of the earlier work (the pair of lovers, the
flute, the dry tree, and the presence of an animal, probably the
same one), but presents them in a darker, more despairing key
which no longer has anything in common with the crystalline
serenity of the *Three Ages*. But the relation between the two can-
vases is, however, much more complex than this, and one is led to
think that Titian has intentionally returned to the work from his
younger years, and in a further investigation of their common
erotic theme has recanted the earlier work point for point (in the
Edinburgh painting—as attested to by the presence of the Erota
and the dry tree—the iconographic theme of the "three ages of
man" is also treated in the form of a meditation on love). First of
all, the figures of the two lovers are inverted; for in the earlier
work, the man is nude and the woman clothed. She, who is represented not from behind but in profile, here holds the flute which
will pass into the hands of the shepherd in the Vienna painting. In
the *Three Ages* we also find, on the right, the shattered and dry
tree—symbol of knowledge and of sin—on which an Eros is lean-
ing; but when taking the motif up again in the late work, Titian
has it blooming on one side, thus bringing together in a single
trunk the two Edenic trees, the Tree of Life and the Tree of
Knowledge of Good and Evil. And while in the *Three Ages* the
fawn is tranquilly stretched on the grass, it now takes the place of
Eros and rises up the Tree of Life.

The enigma of the sexual relationship between the man and the woman, which was already at the center of the first painting, thus receives a new and more mature formulation. Sensual pleasure and love—as the half-bloomed tree bears witness—do not prefigure only death and sin. To be sure, in their fulfillment the lovers learn something of each other that they should not have known—they have lost their mystery—and yet have not become any less impenetrable. But in this mutual disenchantment from their secret, they enter, just as in Benjamin's aphorism, a new and more blessed life, one that is neither animal nor human. It is not nature that is reached in their fulfillment, but rather (as symbolized by the animal that rears up the Tree of Life and of Knowledge) a higher stage beyond both nature and knowledge, beyond concealment and disconcealment. These lovers have initiated each other into their own lack of mystery as their most intimate secret; they mutually forgive each other and expose their *vanitas*. Bare or clothed, they are no longer either concealed or unconcealed—but rather, inapparent {*inapparenti*}. As is clear from both the posture of the two lovers and the flute taken from the lips, their condition is *otium*, it is workless {*senz'opera*}. If it is true, as Dundas writes, that in these paintings Titian has created "a realm in which to reflect on the relationship between body and spirit,"[4] in the Vienna painting this relationship is, so to speak, neutralized. In their fulfillment, the lovers who have lost their mystery contemplate a human nature rendered perfectly inoperative—the inactivity {*inoperosità*} and *desœuvrement* of the human and of the animal as the supreme and unsavable figure of life.

§ 20   Outside of Being

Esotericism means: the articulation of modalities of
non-knowledge.

— Furio Jesi

In Egypt, around the middle of the second century A.D., the
Gnostic Basilides, from whose circle come the animal-headed effigies reproduced by Bataille in *Documents*, composed his exegesis
of the Gospels in twenty books. According to the soteriological
drama that he designs, in the beginning the nonexistent god
issued into the cosmos a triple seed or filial line, the last of which
has remained entangled "like a miscarriage" in the "great heap" of
corporeal matter and must, in the end, make its way back to the
divine nonexistence from which it came. Up to this point nothing
distinguishes Basilides's cosmology from the great Gnostic drama
of cosmic mixture and separation. But what constitutes his incomparable originality is that he is the first to pose the problem of the
state of matter and natural life once all divine or spiritual elements
have abandoned it to return to their original place. And he does
this through a brilliant exegesis of the passage in the Letter to the
Romans in which Paul speaks of the nature that groans and suffers
birth pangs while awaiting redemption:

> When the whole filial line thus arrives above and is beyond the
> boundary of the spirit, then the whole creation will receive compas-
> sion. For up to the present it groans and is tormented and waits for
> the revelation of the sons of God, so that all the men of the filial line
> may go up from here. When that has happened, God will bring on
> the whole world the great ignorance [*megalē agnoia*], so that every

creature may remain in its natural condition [*kata physin*] and none desire anything contrary to its nature. Thus, all the souls who find themselves in this expanse, whose nature it is to remain immortal in this place alone, will stay here below, knowing nothing other than or better than this expanse; in the regions below there will be no news and no knowledge of the realities above, so that the souls below may not be tormented by desiring impossible things, like fish striving to graze on the hills with the sheep—for such a desire would be their destruction.[1]

In the idea of this natural life that is unsavable and that has been completely abandoned by every spiritual element—and yet, because of the "great ignorance," is nonetheless perfectly blessed—Basilides has thought a sort of grand counterimage of man's regained animality at the end of history, which so bothered Bataille. Here darkness and light, matter and spirit, animal life and *logos* (the articulation of which in the anthropological machine produced the human) are separated forever. But not in order to close themselves in a more impenetrable mystery; rather, to liberate their own truer nature. A critic has written apropos of Jarry that one of the alchemical keys to his work appears to be "the belief, inherited from medieval science, that the man who managed to separate the different natures tightly bound together during his existence would succeed in freeing within himself the profound sense of life."[2] It is not easy to think this figure—whether new or very ancient—of the life that shines in the "saved night" of nature's (and, in particular, human nature's) eternal, unsavable survival after it has definitively bid farewell to the *logos* and to its own history. It is no longer human, because it has perfectly forgotten every rational element, every project for mastering its animal life; but if animality had been defined precisely by its poverty in world and by its obscure expectation of a revelation and a salvation, then this life cannot be called animal either. It surely "does not see the open," in the sense that it does not appropriate it as an instrument of mastery and knowledge; but neither does it remain simply closed in its own captivation. The *agnoia*, the nonknowledge which has descended upon it, does not entail the loss of every

Can observe the Open, but cannot access, touch, or master it. Trapped in thrall of the open?

relation to its own concealment. Rather, this life remains serenely in relation with its own proper nature (*menei . . . kata physin*) as a zone of nonknowledge.

Etymologists have always been left perplexed when faced with the Latin verb *ignoscere*, which seems explicable as **in-gnosco*, yet which does not mean "not to know" {*ignorare*}, but rather "to forgive." To articulate a zone of nonknowledge—or better, of a-knowledge {*ignoscenza*}[3]—means in this sense not simply to let something be, but to leave something outside of being, to render it unsavable. Just as Titian's lovers forgive each other for their own lack of mystery, so in the saved night, life—neither open nor undisconcealable—stands serenely in relation with its own concealedness; it lets it be outside of being.

In Heidegger's interpretation, the animal can relate itself to its disinhibitor neither as a being nor as a nonbeing because only with man is the disinhibitor for the first time allowed to be as such; only with man can there be something like being, and beings become accessible and manifest. Thus, the supreme category of Heidegger's ontology is stated: letting be. In this project, man makes himself free for the possible, and in delivering himself over to it, lets the world and beings be as such. However, if our reading has hit the mark, if man can open a world and free a possibile only because, in the experience of boredom, he is able to suspend and deactivate the animal relationship with the disinhibitor, if at the center of the open lies the undisconcealedness of the animal, then at this point we must ask: what becomes of this relationship? In what way can man let the animal, upon whose suspension the world is held open, be?

Insofar as the animal knows neither beings nor nonbeings, neither open nor closed, it is outside of being; it is outside in an exteriority more external than any open, and inside in an intimacy more internal than any closedness. To let the animal be would then mean: to let it be *outside of being*. The zone of nonknowledge—or of a-knowledge—that is at issue here is beyond both knowing and not knowing, beyond both disconcealing and concealing, beyond both being and the nothing. But what is thus left to be outside of being is not thereby negated or taken away; it is not, for this reason, inexistent. It is an existing, real thing that has gone beyond the difference between being and beings.

However, it is not here a question of trying to trace the no longer human or animal contours of a new creation that would run the risk of being equally as mythological as the other. As we have seen, in our culture man has always been the result of a simultaneous division and articulation of the animal and the human, in which one of the two terms of the operation was also what was at stake in it. To render inoperative the machine that governs our conception of man will therefore mean no longer to seek new—more effective or more authentic—articulations, but rather to show the central emptiness, the hiatus that—within man—separates man and animal, and to risk ourselves in this emptiness: the suspension of the suspension, Shabbat of both animal and man.

And if one day, according to a now-classic image, the "face in the sand" that the sciences of man have formed on the shore of our history should finally be erased, what will appear in its place will not be a new *mandylion* or "Veronica" of a regained humanity or animality. The righteous with animal heads in the miniature in the Ambrosian do not represent a new declension of the man-animal relation so much as a figure of the "great ignorance" which lets both of them be outside of being, saved precisely in their being unsavable. Perhaps there is still a way in which living beings can sit at the messianic banquet of the righteous without taking on a historical task and without setting the anthropological machine into action. Once again, the solution of the *mysterium coniunctionis* by which the human has been produced passes through an unprecedented inquiry into the practico-political mystery of separation.

Notes

Chapter 1

1. Zofia Ameisenowa, "Animal-Headed Gods, Evangelists, Saints and Righteous Men," *Journal of the Warburg and Courtauld Institutes* 12 (1949): 21–45.

2. An English version of this text is found in James H. Charlesworth, ed., *The Old Testament Pseudepigrapha*, vol. 1, *Apocalyptic Literature and Testaments* (Garden City, N.J.: Doubleday, 1983), 630.

3. Henri-Charles Puech, *Sur le manichéisme et autres essais* (Paris: Flammarion, 1979), 105.

Chapter 2

1. See Georges Bataille, "Base Materialism and Gnosticism," in *Visions of Excess*, ed. Allan Stoekl, trans. Allan Stoekl with Carl R. Lovitt and Donald M. Leslie, Jr. (Minneapolis: University of Minnesota Press, 1985), 45–52; original in Bataille, "Le bas matérialisme et la gnose," in *Œuvres complètes*, vol. 1, *Premiers écrits, 1922–1940* (Paris: Gallimard, 1970), 220–26.

2. Bataille, "The Sacred Conspiracy," in *Visions of Excess*, 181; original in Bataille, "La conjuration sacrée," in *Œuvres complètes*, vol. 1, 445.

3. Alexandre Kojève, *Introduction to the Reading of Hegel*, ed. Allan Bloom, trans. James H. Nichols, Jr. (Ithaca, N.Y.: Cornell University Press, 1980), 158–59; original in Kojève, *Introduction à la lecture de Hegel* (1947; Paris: Gallimard, 1979), 434–35.

4. Denis Hollier, ed., *The College of Sociology (1937–39)*, trans. Betsy

Wing (Minneapolis: University of Minnesota Press, 1988), 90; original in Hollier, ed., *Le Collège de Sociologie (1937–1939)* (Paris: Gallimard, 1979), 171.

    5. Ibid., 45; original, 103.

Chapter 3

    1. Kojève, 159; original, 436.
    2. Ibid., 161; original, 436–37.
    3. Ibid.; original, 437.
    4. Ibid., 161–62; original, 437.
    5. Kojève, *Introduction à la lecture de Hegel,* 554.

Chapter 4

    1. Aristotle's terms here are *empsychon* and *apsychon.* Agamben translates them as *l'animale* and *l'inanimato,* which clearly show their derivation from the Latin and Italian word *anima,* or "soul."

    2. Aristotle, *De anima,* 413a, 20–413b, 8; English version in *The Complete Works of Aristotle,* ed. Jonathan Barnes (Princeton: Princeton University Press, 1984), 658.

    3. Xavier Bichat, *Physiological Researches on Life and Death,* trans. F. Gold (Boston: Richardson and Lord, 1827), 13; original in Bichat, *Recherches physiologiques sur la vie et la mort* (1800; Paris: Flammarion, 1994), 61.

Chapter 5

    1. Iohannis Scotti Eriugenae [John Scotus Erigena], *Periphyseon (De divisione naturae). Liber quartus,* ed. Édouard A. Jeauneau, trans. John J. O'Meara and I. P. Sheldon-Williams (Dublin: Dublin Institute for Advanced Studies, 1995), 188–91.

    2. Thomas Aquinas, *The "Summa Theologica" of St. Thomas Aquinas,* vol. 20, *Part III (Supplement) QQ. 69–86,* trans. Fathers of the English Dominican Province (London: Burns Oates and Washbourne, 1912), 193; original in Aquinas, *Somme théologique. La Résurrection,* ed. Jean-Dominique Folghera (Paris—Rome: Desclée, 1955), 151–52.

    3. Aquinas, *The "Summa Theologica,"* vol. 21, *Part III (Supplement) QQ. 87–99,* 68; original in Aquinas, *Somme théologique. Le monde des ressuscités,* ed. Réginald-Omez (Paris and Rome: Desclée, 1961), 153.

Chapter 6

1. Aquinas, *The "Summa Theologica,"* vol. 4, *Part I, QQ. 75–102,*
328–329; original in Aquinas, *Somme théologique. Les Origines de*
l'homme, ed. Albert Patfoort (Paris and Rome: Desclée, 1963), 193.

Chapter 7

1. Carolus Linnaeus [Carl von Linné], *Menniskans Cousiner,* ed.
Telemak Fredbärj (Uppsala: Ekenäs, 1955), 4–5.
2. Edward Tyson, *Orang-Outang, sive Homo Sylvestris: or, the*
Anatomy of a Pygmie Compared with that of a Monkey, an Ape, and a
Man. To which is added, a Philological Essay Concerning the Pygmies, the
Cynocephali, the Satyrs, and Sphinges of the Ancients. Wherein it Will
Appear that They are all Either Apes or Monkeys, and not Men, as Formerly
Pretended (London: Bennet and Brown, 1699), n. p.
3. Carolus Linnaeus, *Systema naturae, sive, Regna tria naturae system-*
atice proposita per classes, ordines, genera, & species (Lugduni Batavorum:
Haak, 1735), 6.
4. Johann Georg Gmelin, *Reliquiae quae supersunt commercii epis-*
tolici cum Carolo Linnaeo, Alberto Hallero, Guilielmo Stellero et al. . . . ,
ed. G. H. Theodor Plieninger (Stuttgartiae: Academia Scientiarum
Caesarea Petropolitana, 1861), 55.

Chapter 8

1. Giovanni Pico della Mirandola, *On the Dignity of Man,* trans.
Charles Glenn Wallis (Indianapolis: Hackett, 1998), 4; original in Pico
della Mirandola, *Oratio/Discorso,* ed. Saverio Marchignoli, in Pier Cesare
Bori, *Pluralità delle vie. Alle origini del "Discorso" sulla dignità umana di*
Pico della Mirandola (Milano: Feltrinelli, 2000), 102.
2. Ibid.
3. Ibid., 5; original, 102–4.
4. Ibid.; original, 104
5. Ibid.
6. James Burnett, Lord Monboddo, Preface to Charles-Marie de la
Condamine, *An Account of a Savage Girl, Caught Wild in the Woods of*
Champagne (Aberdeen: Burnett and Rettie, 1796), xviii.
7. Denis Diderot, *"Rameau's Nephew" and "d'Alembert's Dream,"*

trans. Leonard Tancock (Harmondsworth: Penguin, 1966), 175–76; original in Diderot, *Le Rêve de d'Alembert*, ed. Jean Varloot and Georges Dulac, in *Œuvres complètes*, vol. 17, *Idées 4. Principes philosophiques sur la matière et le mouvement. Le Rêve de d'Alembert. Éléments de physiologie*, ed. Herbert Dieckmann and Jean Varloot (Paris: Hermann, 1987), 130.

Chapter 9

1. Ernst Haeckel, *The Riddle of the Universe*, trans. Joseph McCabe (New York and London: Harper and Brothers, 1900), 82; original in Haeckel, *Die Welträtsel. Gemeinverständliche Studien über monistische Philosophie* (Stuttgart: Kröner, 1899), 37.

2. Ibid., 83–84; original, 37.

3. Ibid., 87; original, 39.

4. Heymann Steinthal, *Abriss der Sprachwissenschaft, 1: Einleitung in die Psychologie und Sprachwissenschaft* (1871; Berlin: Dümmler, 1881), 355–56.

5. Heymann Steinthal, *Der Ursprung der Sprache im Zusammenhange mit den letzten Fragen alles Wissens. Eine Darstellung, Kritik und Fortentwicklung der vorzüglichsten Ansichten* (1851; Berlin: Dümmler, 1877), 303.

Chapter 11

1. Jakob von Uexküll and Georg Kriszat, *Streifzüge durch die Umwelten von Tieren und Menschen. Ein Bilderbuch unsichtbarer Welten* (1934; Hamburg: Rowohlt, 1956), 85–86.

2. Ibid., 86–87.

3. Ibid., 98.

Chapter 12

1. Martin Heidegger, *Being and Time*, trans. John Macquarrie and Edward Robinson (New York: Harper and Row, 1962), 75; original in Heidegger, *Sein und Zeit* (1927; Tübingen: Niemeyer, 1972), 87.

2. Martin Heidegger, *The Fundamental Concepts of Metaphysics: World, Finitude, Solitiude*, trans. William McNeill and Nicholas Walker (Bloomington: Indiana University Press, 1995), 263; original in Heidegger, *Gesamtausgabe*, vol. 29–30, *Die Grundbegriffe der Metaphysik. Welt—Endlichkeit—Einsamkeit* (Frankfurt a. M.: Klostermann, 1983), 383.

3. Ibid., 254; original, 369.
4. Ibid., 238–39; original, 347–48.
5. Ibid., 242; original, 352–53.
6. Ibid., 247; original, 360.
7. Ibid., 247–48; original, 360.
8. Ibid., 248; original, 361.
9. Ibid.; original, 361–62.
10. Ibid., 253; original, 368.
11. Ibid., 269–70; original, 391–92.

Chapter 13

1. Martin Heidegger, *Parmenides*, trans. André Schuwer and Richard Rojcewicz (Bloomington: Indiana University Press, 1992), 150; original in Heidegger, *Gesamtausgabe*, vol. 44, *Parmenides*, ed. Manfred S. Frings (Frankfurt a. M.: Klostermann, 1993), 224.
2. Ibid., 155; original, 231.
3. Ibid., 152; original, 226.
4. Ibid., 159–60; original, 237.
5. Ibid., 160; original, 237–38.
6. Ibid.; original, 239.
7. Ibid., 160–61; original, 239.
8. Heidegger, *Fundamental Concepts*, 255; original, 371–72.
9. Ibid., 272–73; original, 395–96.
10. Ibid., 282; original, 408.
11. Agamben here translates Heidegger's *Stimmung* as *stato d'animo* or "state of mind." *Stimmung*—which is related to *Stimme* ("voice") and *stimmen* ("to tune [an instrument]," "to be in tune," "to accord")—also carries the meanings of "(musical) pitch," "(musical) key," "disposition," "feeling." Macquarrie and Robinson translate it as "mood." I have retained McNeill and Walker's "attunement." Agamben also occasionally refers to it as an "emotional tonality."
12. Ibid., 282; original, 409.

Chapter 14

1. Heidegger, *Fundamental Concepts*, 93; original, 140.
2. Ibid., 101; original, 153.
3. Ibid., 102; original, 154.
4. Ibid., 92; original, 138.

5. Ibid., 138–39; original, 208–10.

6. Ibid., 140–41; original, 212.

7. Ibid., 143–44; original, 215–16.

8. Heidegger, *Parmenides*, 13; original, 19.

9. Ibid., 15–16; original, 22.

10. Martin Heidegger, "What Is Metaphysics?" trans. David Farrell Krell, in *Pathmarks*, ed. William McNeill (Cambridge: Cambridge University Press, 1998), 91; original in Heidegger, *Wegmarken* (Frankfurt a. M.: Klostermann, 1967), 12.

11. Ibid., 96; original, 18.

12. Ibid., 90; original, 11.

Chapter 15

1. Martin Heidegger, "The Origin of the Work of Art," in *Poetry, Language, Thought*, trans. Albert Hofstadter (New York: Harper and Row, 1971), 43; original in Heidegger, "Der Ursprung des Kunstwerkes," in *Holzwege* (Frankfurt a. M.: Klostermann, 1950), 30.

2. Ibid., 46; original, 32.

3. Ibid.

4. Ibid., 45; original, 31.

5. Ibid., 46; original, 32.

6. Ibid., 47; original, 33–34.

7. Ibid., 47–48; original, 34.

8. Heidegger, *Parmenides*, 90; original, 133.

9. Martin Heidegger, "Letter on 'Humanism,'" trans. Frank A. Capuzzi, in *Pathmarks*, 247; original in Heidegger, "Brief über den 'Humanismus,'" in *Wegmarken*, 155.

Chapter 16

1. Martin Heidegger, *Gesamtausgabe*, vol. 39, *Hölderlins Hymnen "Germanien" und "Der Rhein,"* ed. Susanne Ziegler (Frankfurt a. M.: Klostermann, 1980), 99.

Chapter 18

1. Benjamin to Florens Christian Rang, December 9, 1923, trans. Rodney Livingstone, in Walter Benjamin, *Selected Writings*, vol. 1, *1913–1926*, ed. Marcus Bullock and Michael W. Jennings (Cambridge: Harvard University Press, Belknap Press, 1996), 389; original in

Benjamin, *Gesammelte Briefe*, vol. 2, *1919–1924*, ed. Christoph Gödde and Henri Lonitz (Frankfurt a. M.: Suhrkamp, 1996), 393.

2. Walter Benjamin, "Theological-Political Fragment," in *Reflections*, ed. Peter Demetz, trans. Edmund Jephcott (New York: Schocken, 1986), 313; original in Benjamin, "Theologisch-politisches Fragment," in *Gesammelte Schriften*, vol. 2:1, ed. Rolf Tiedemann and Hermann Schweppenhäuser (Frankfurt a. M.: Suhrkamp, 1980), 172.

3. Walter Benjamin, "One-Way Street," trans. Edmund Jephcott, in *Selected Writings*, vol. 1, 487; original in Benjamin, *Einbahnstraße*, in *Gesammelte Schriften*, vol. 4:1, 68.

4. Ibid., 482; original, 62.

Chapter 19

1. Erwin Panofsky, *Problems in Titian, Mostly Iconographic* (New York: New York University Press, 1969), 169.

2. Ibid.

3. Judith Dundas, "A Titian Enigma," *Artibus et Historiae* 12 (1985): 54.

4. Ibid., 55.

Chapter 20

1. Werner Foerster, ed., *Gnosis: A Selection of Gnostic Texts*, vol. 1, *Patristic Evidence* (Oxford: Clarendon Press, 1972), 72; original in Manilio Simonetti, ed., *Testi gnostici in lingua greca e latina* (Milano: Mondadori, 1993), 172.

2. René Massat, Preface to Alfred Jarry, *Œuvres complètes*, vol. 1 (Lausanne and Monte Carlo: Édition du Livre, 1948), 12.

3. "A-knowledge" is an attempt to render Agamben's neologism *ignoscenza*, which he of course derives from the Latin verb *ignoscere*. In addition to meaning "not knowing," the word would thus also carry the sense of "forgiveness" or "pardon," and might best be understood as a sort of "forgetful forgiveness."

Index of Names

MERIDIAN

Crossing Aesthetics

Hans-Jost Frey, *Studies in Poetic Discourse: Mallarmé, Baudelaire, Rimbaud, Hölderlin*

Pierre Bourdieu, *The Rules of Art: Genesis and Structure of the Literary Field*

Nicolas Abraham, *Rhythms: On the Work, Translation, and Psychoanalysis*

Jacques Derrida, *On the Name*

David Wills, *Prosthesis*

Maurice Blanchot, *The Work of Fire*

Jacques Derrida, *Points . . . : Interviews, 1974–1994*

J. Hillis Miller, *Topographies*

Philippe Lacoue-Labarthe, *Musica Ficta (Figures of Wagner)*

Jacques Derrida, *Aporias*

Emmanuel Levinas, *Outside the Subject*

Jean-François Lyotard, *Lessons on the Analytic of the Sublime*

Peter Fenves, *"Chatter": Language and History in Kierkegaard*

Jean-Luc Nancy, *The Experience of Freedom*

Jean-Joseph Goux, *Oedipus, Philosopher*

Haun Saussy, *The Problem of a Chinese Aesthetic*

Jean-Luc Nancy, *The Birth to Presence*